FOR ORGANS, PIANOS & ELECTRONIC KEYBOARDS

E-Z PLAY® TODAY

142

CLASSIC JAZZ

ISBN 978-1-4584-1413-7

HAL•LEONARD®
CORPORATION
7777 W. BLUEMOUND RD. P.O. BOX 13819 MILWAUKEE, WI 53213

Visit Hal Leonard Online at
www.halleonard.com

CONTENTS

All Blues

Registration 7
Rhythm: Jazz Waltz or Waltz

By Miles Davis

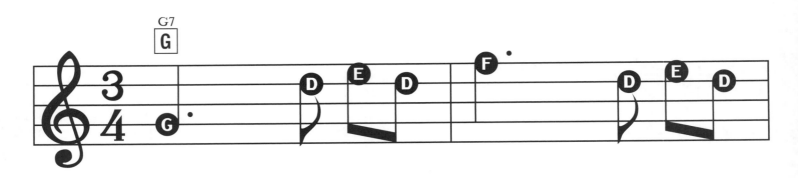

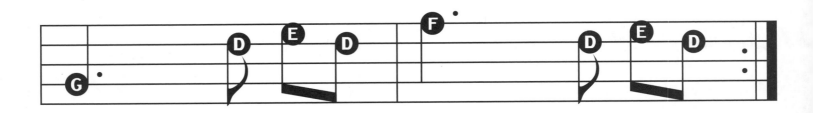

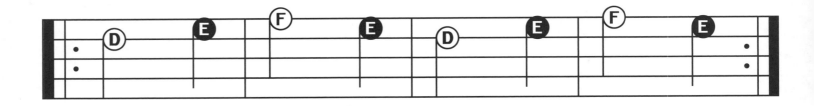

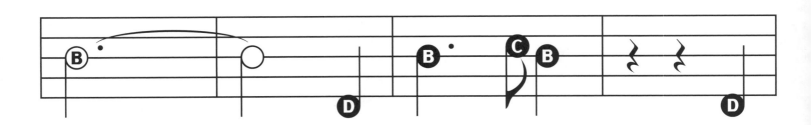

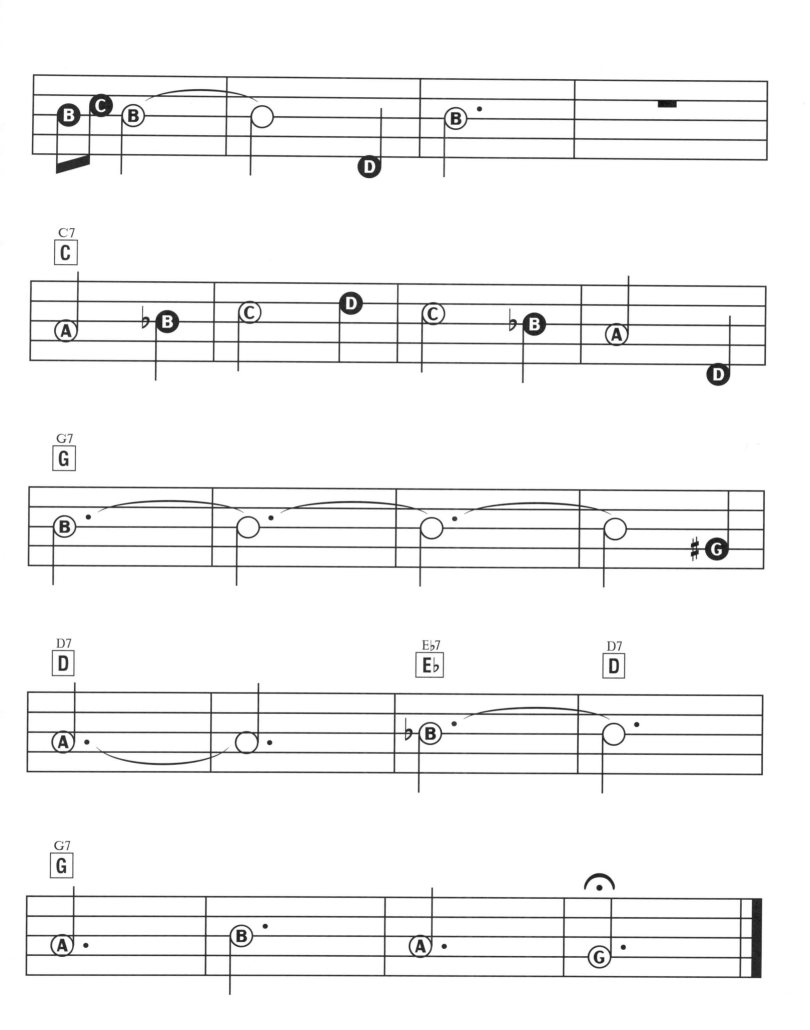

Au Privave

Registration 8
Rhythm: Swing

By Charlie Parker

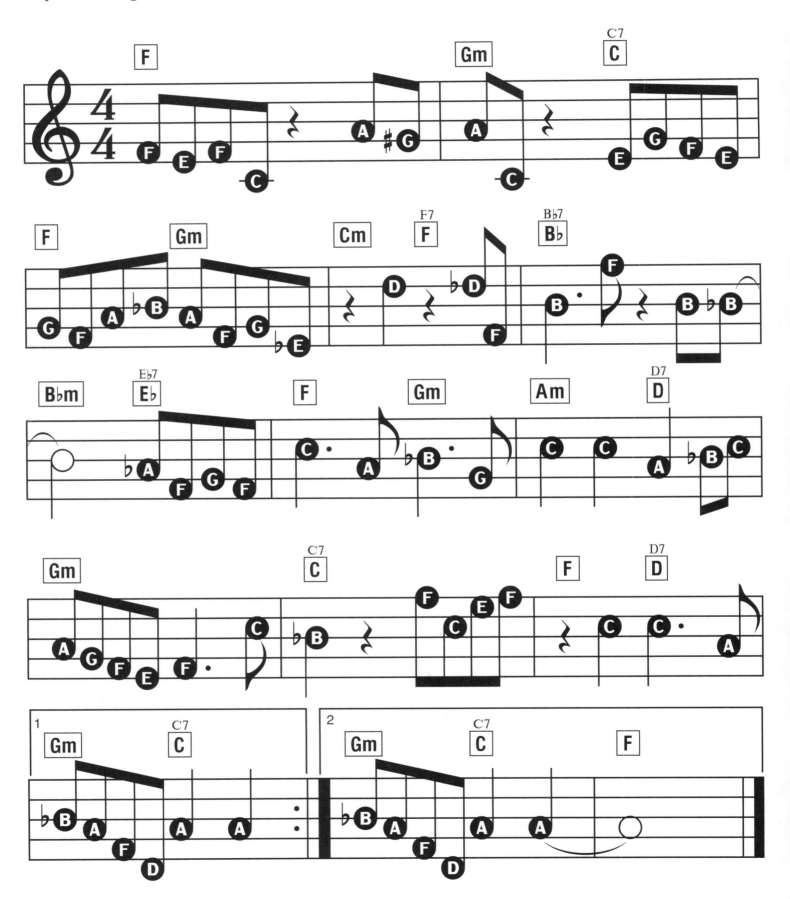

C-Jam Blues

Registration 8
Rhythm: Swing

By Duke Ellington

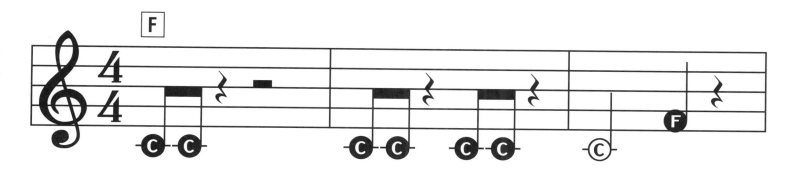

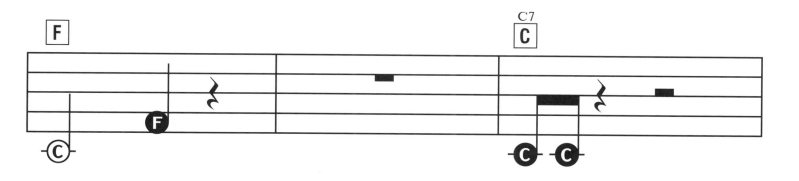

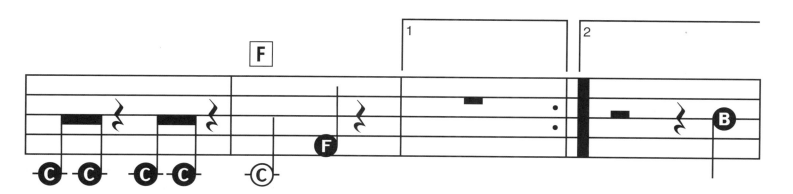

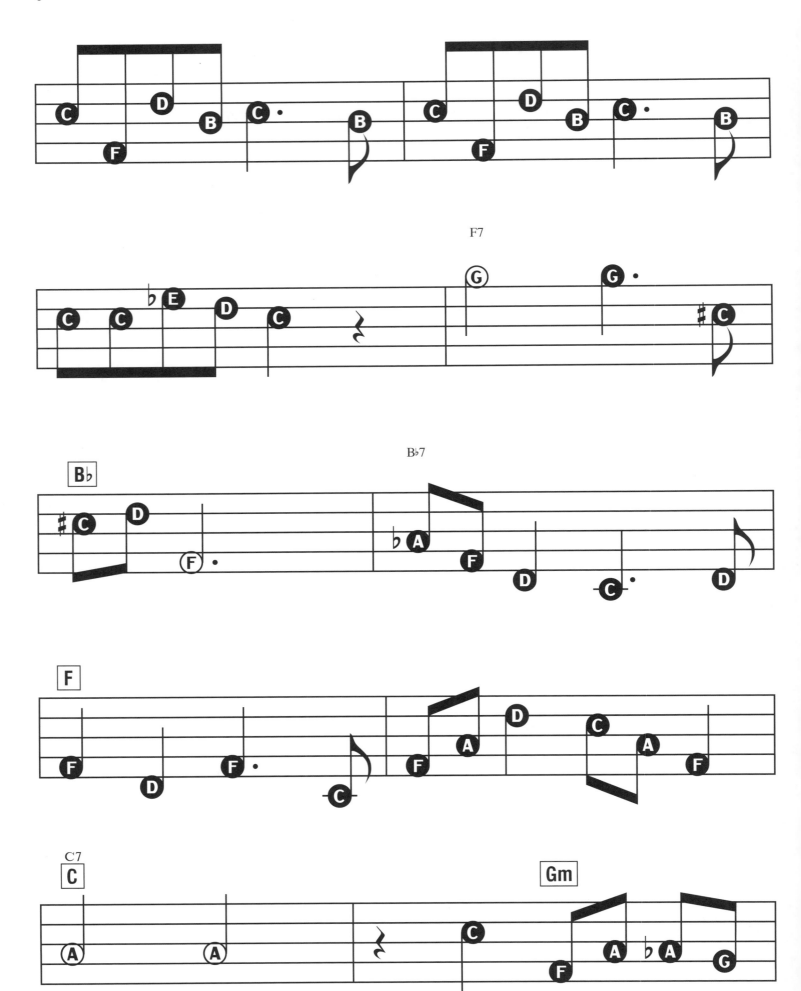

9

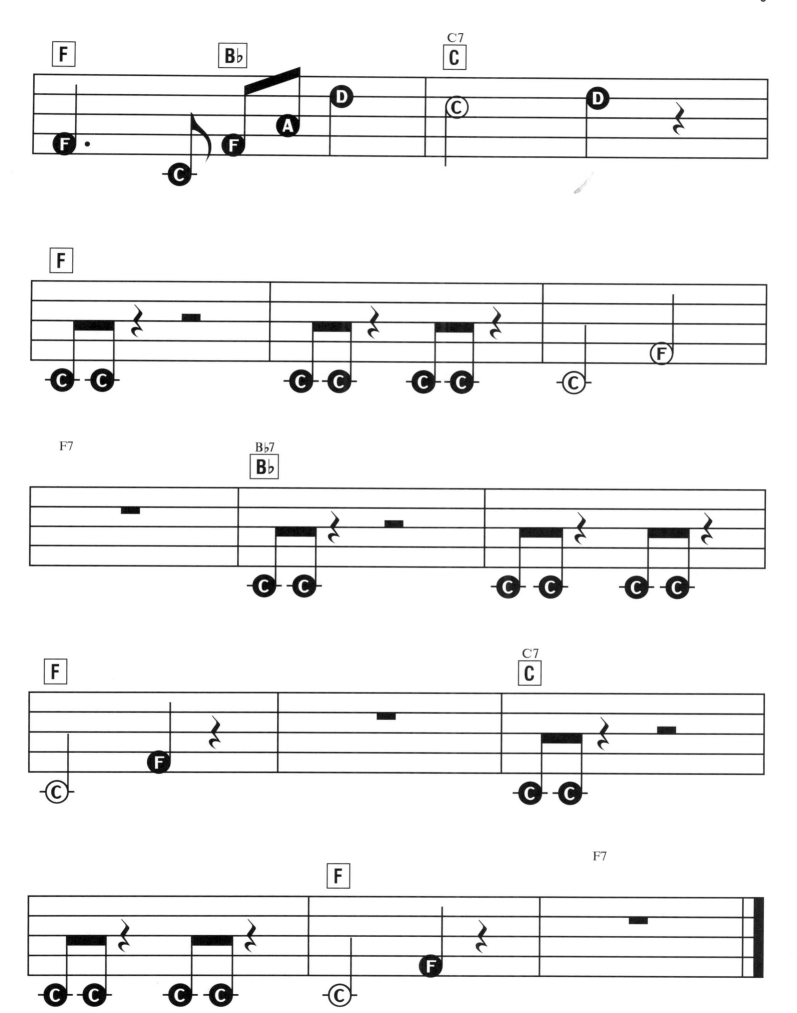

Bag's New Groove

Registration 5
Rhythm: Swing

By Milt Jackson

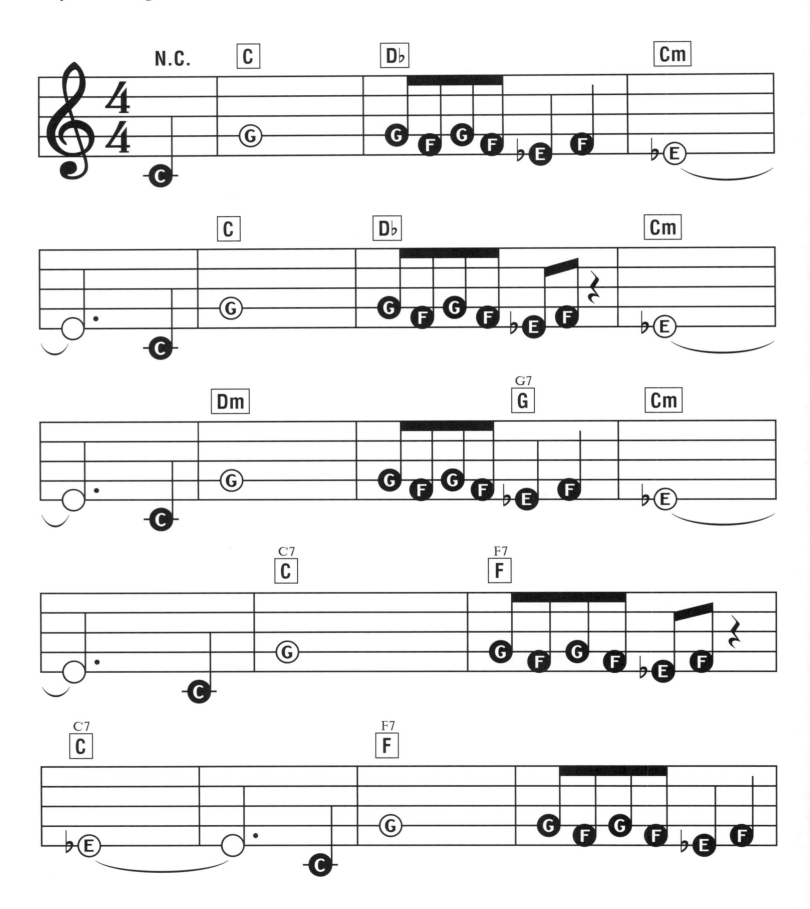

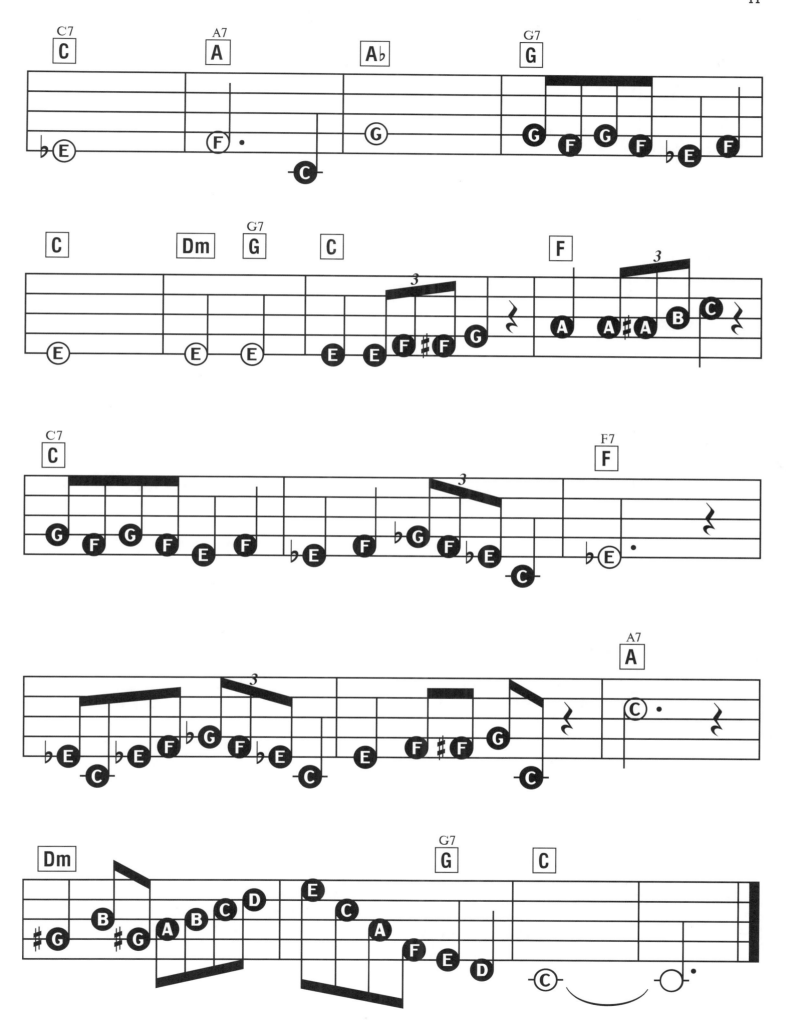

Billie's Bounce
(Bill's Bounce)

Registration 2
Rhythm: Swing

By Charlie Parker

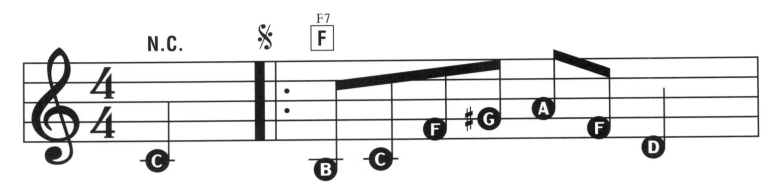

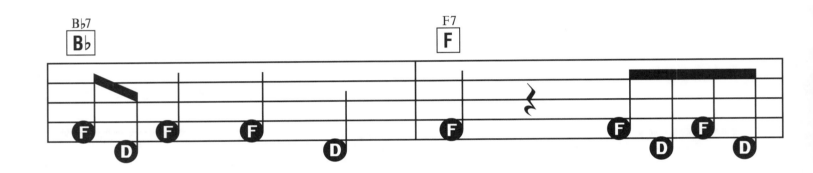

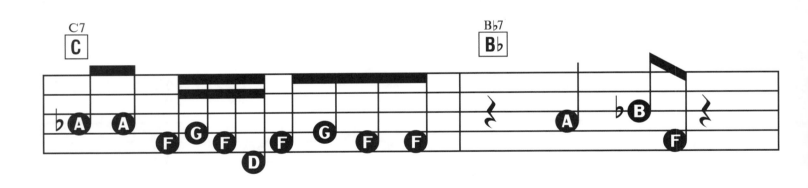

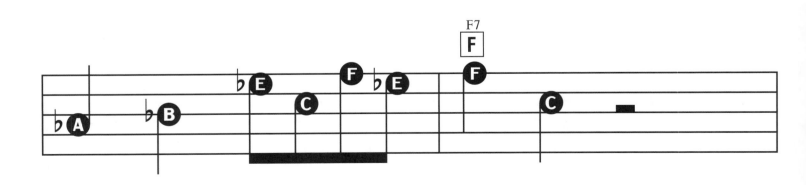

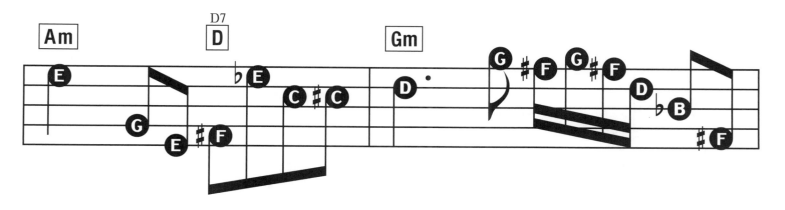

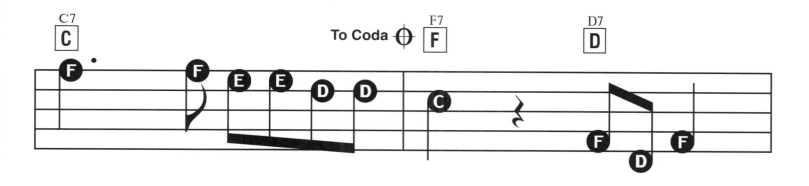

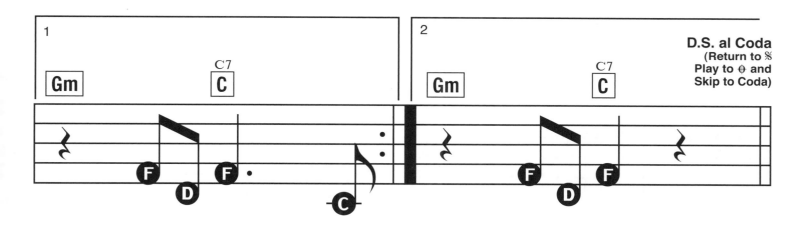

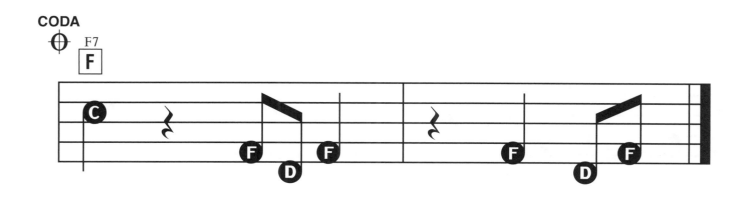

Bluesology

Registration 8
Rhythm: Swing

By Milt Jackson

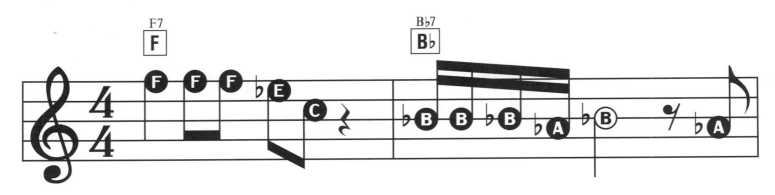

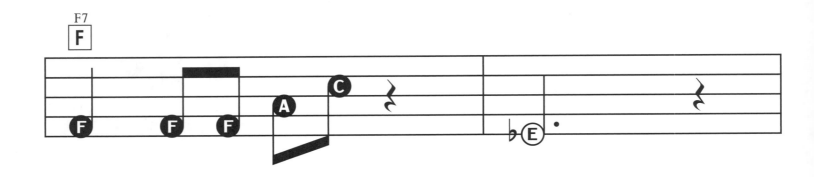

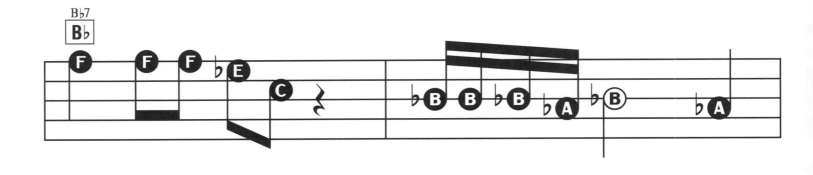

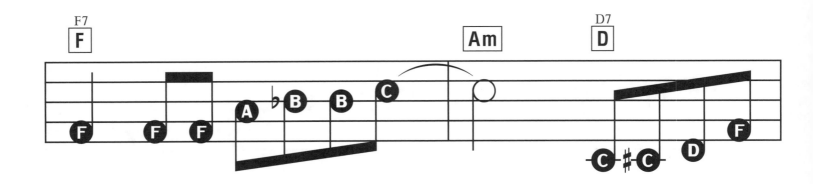

15

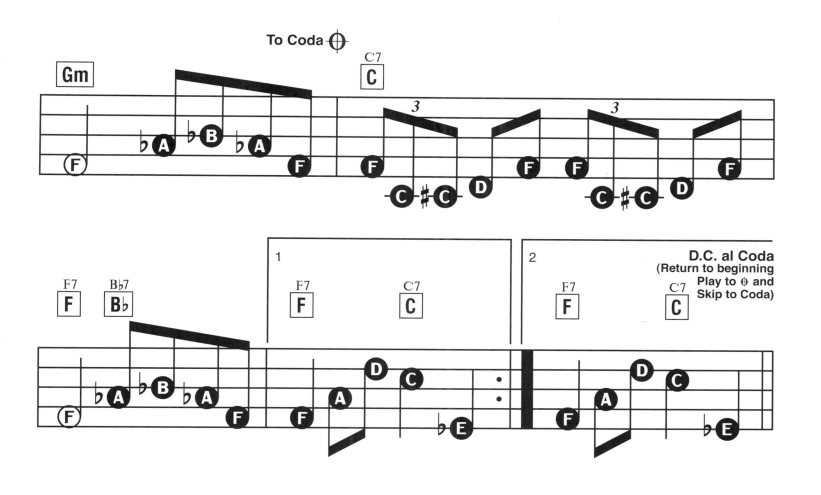

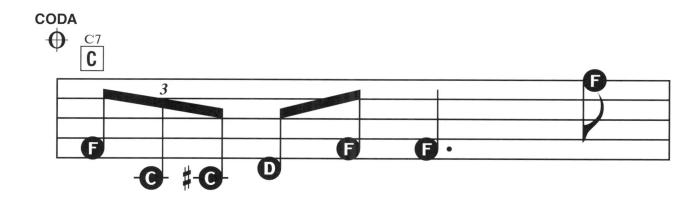

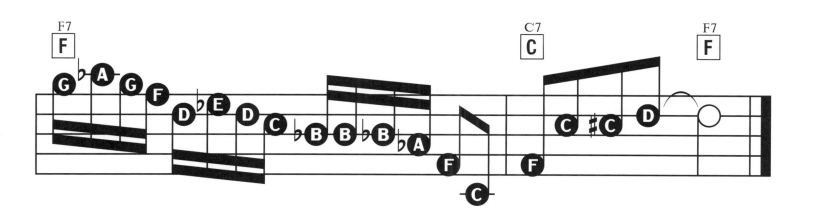

A Child Is Born

Registration 2
Rhythm: Waltz

By Thad Jones

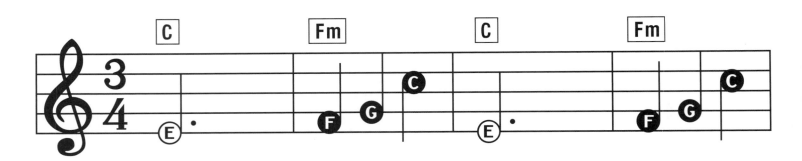

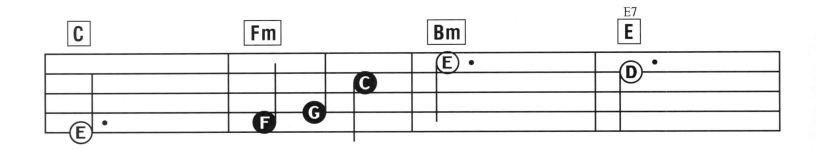

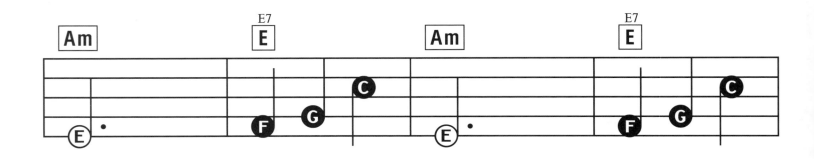

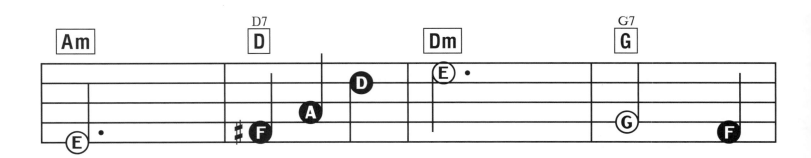

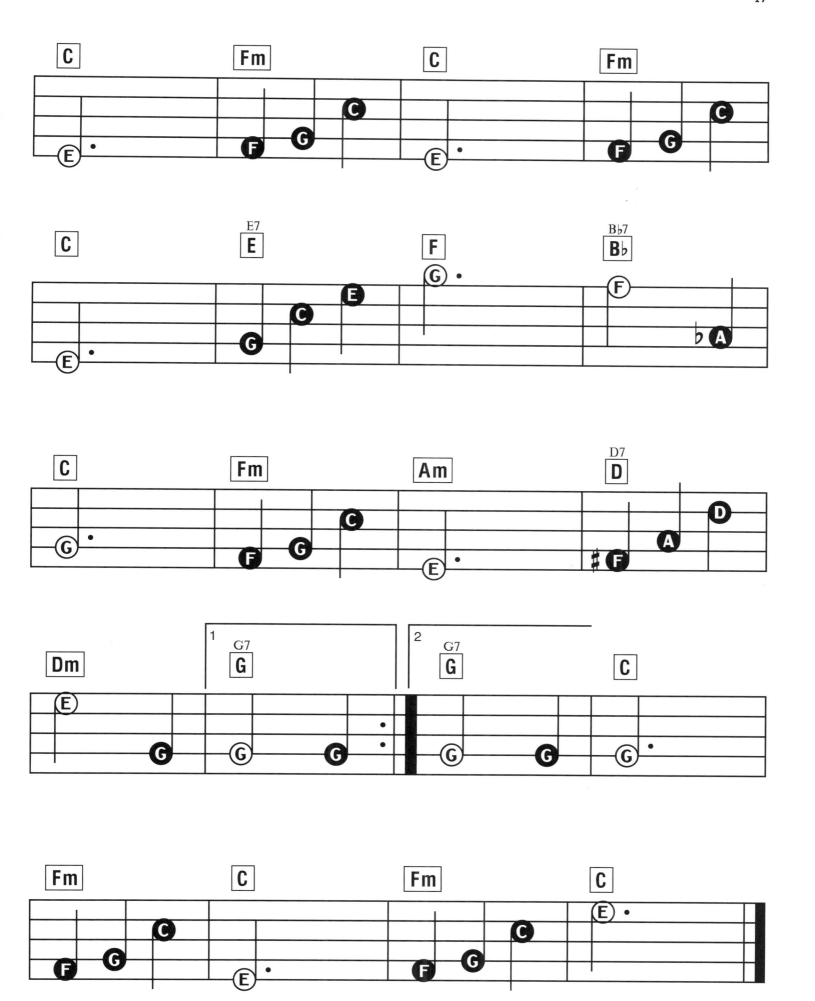

Dear Old Stockholm

Registration 2
Rhythm: Swing

Swedish Folksong

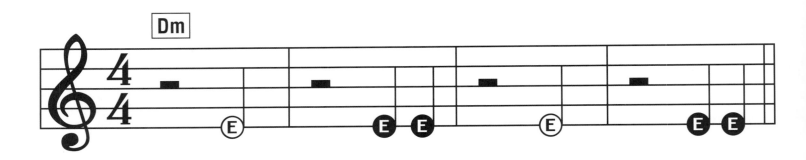

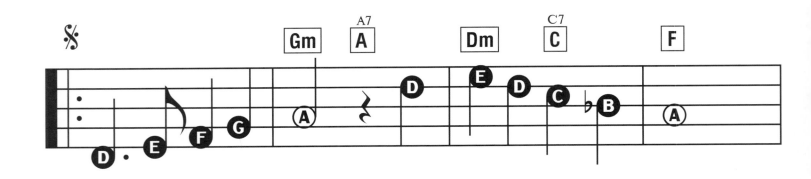

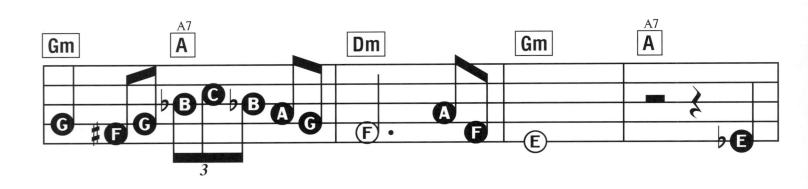

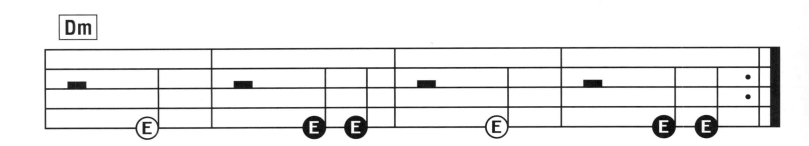

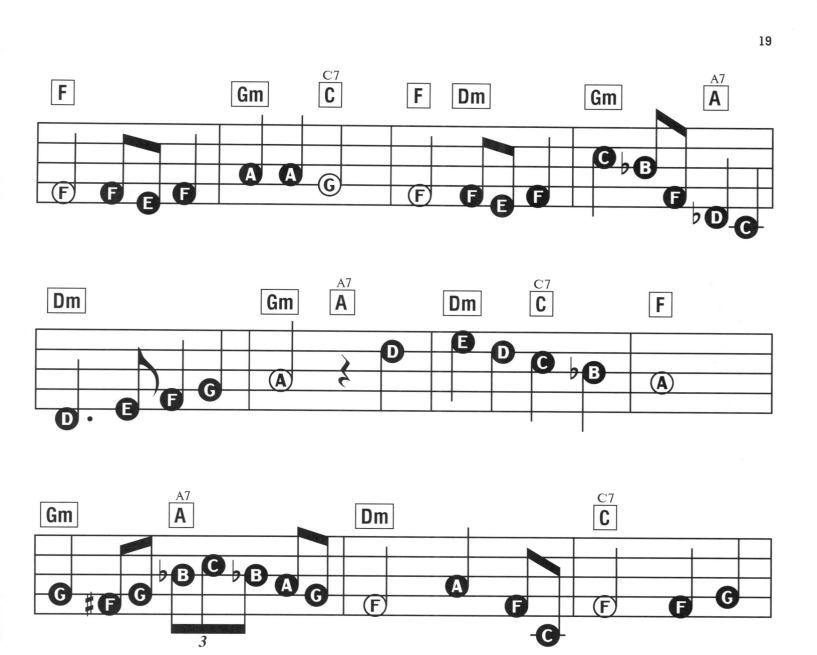

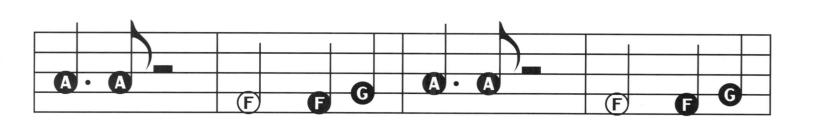

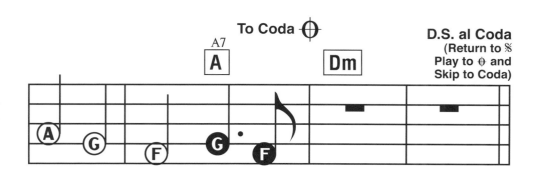

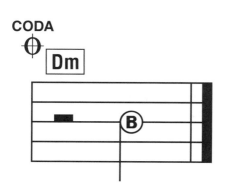

Detour Ahead

Registration 8
Rhythm: Ballad or Swing

By Herb Ellis,
John Frigo and Lou Carter

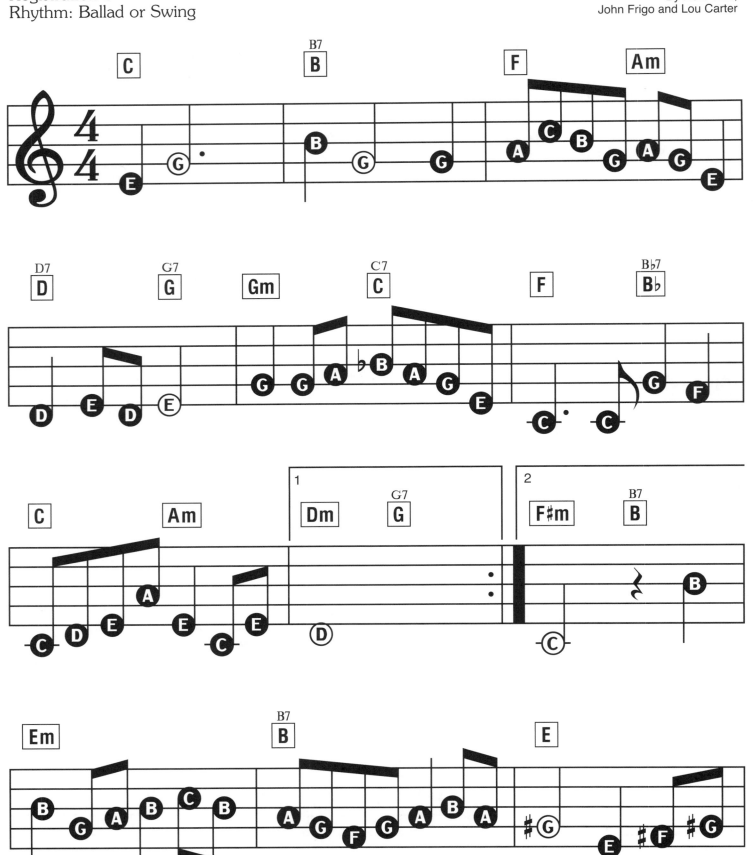

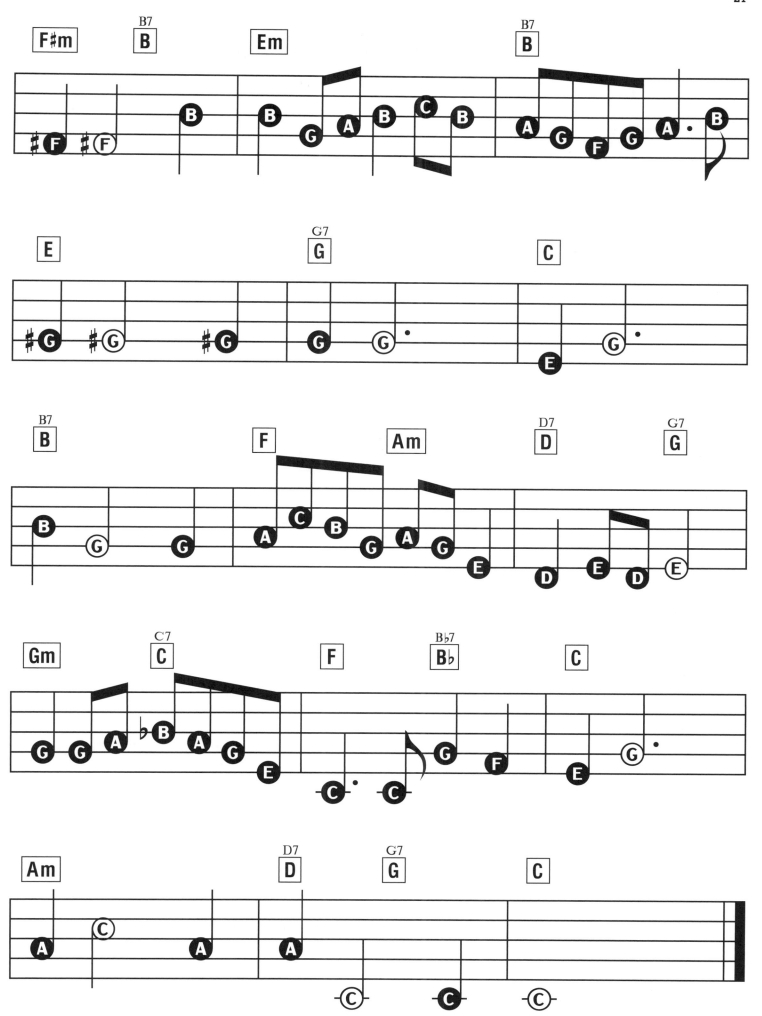

Django

Registration 8
Rhythm: Swing

By John Lewis

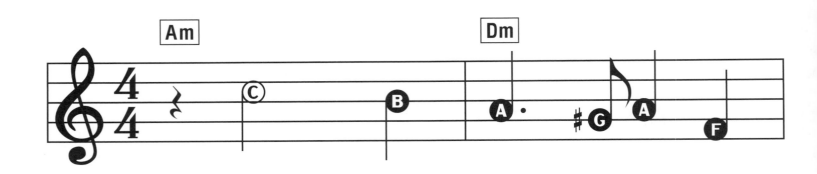

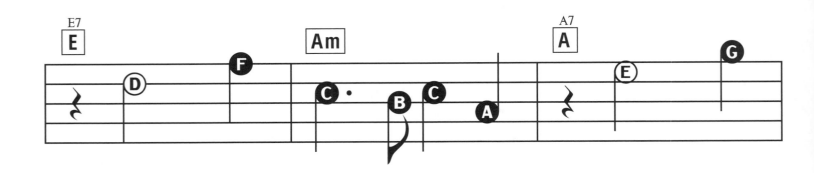

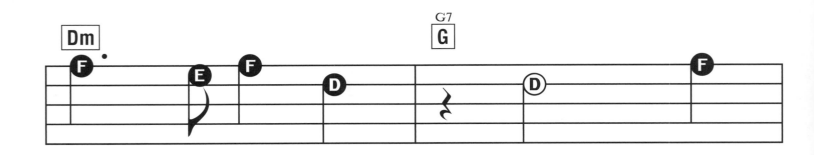

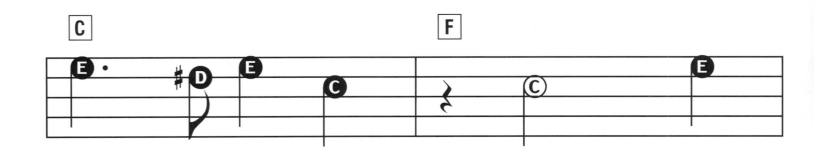

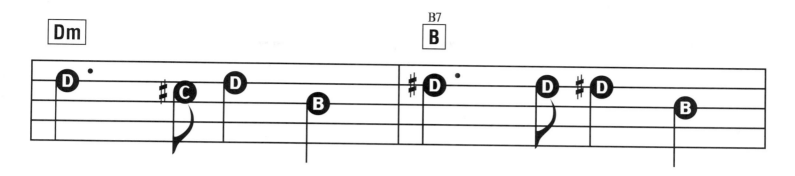

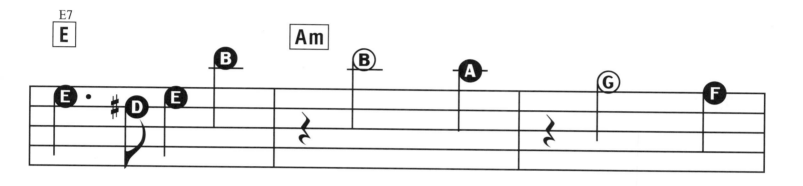

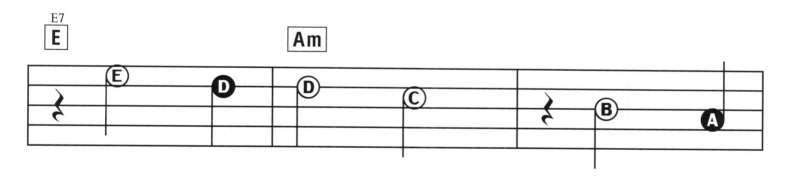

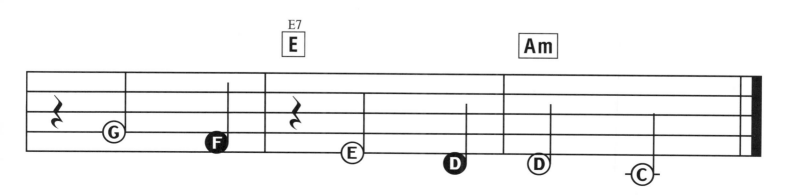

Estate

Registration 4
Rhythm: Bossa Nova or Latin

Music by Bruno Martino
Lyrics by Bruno Brighetti

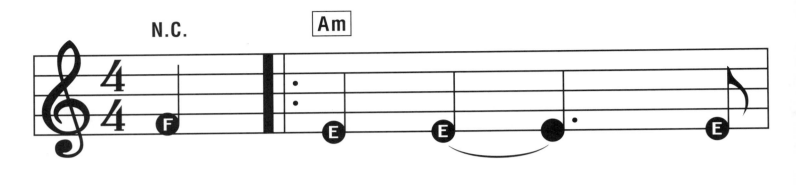

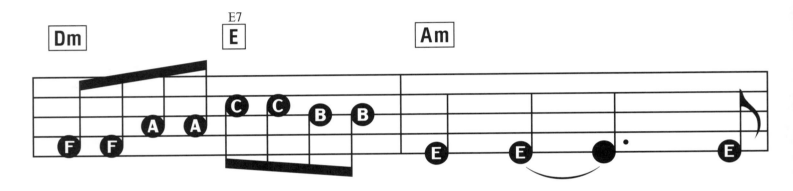

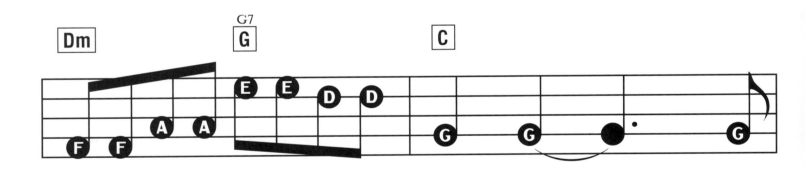

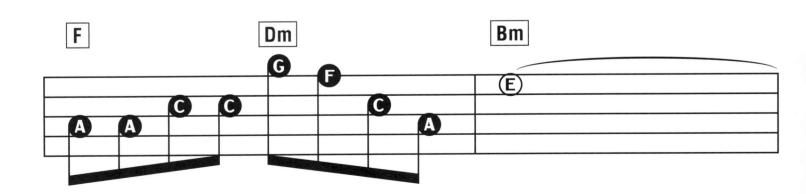

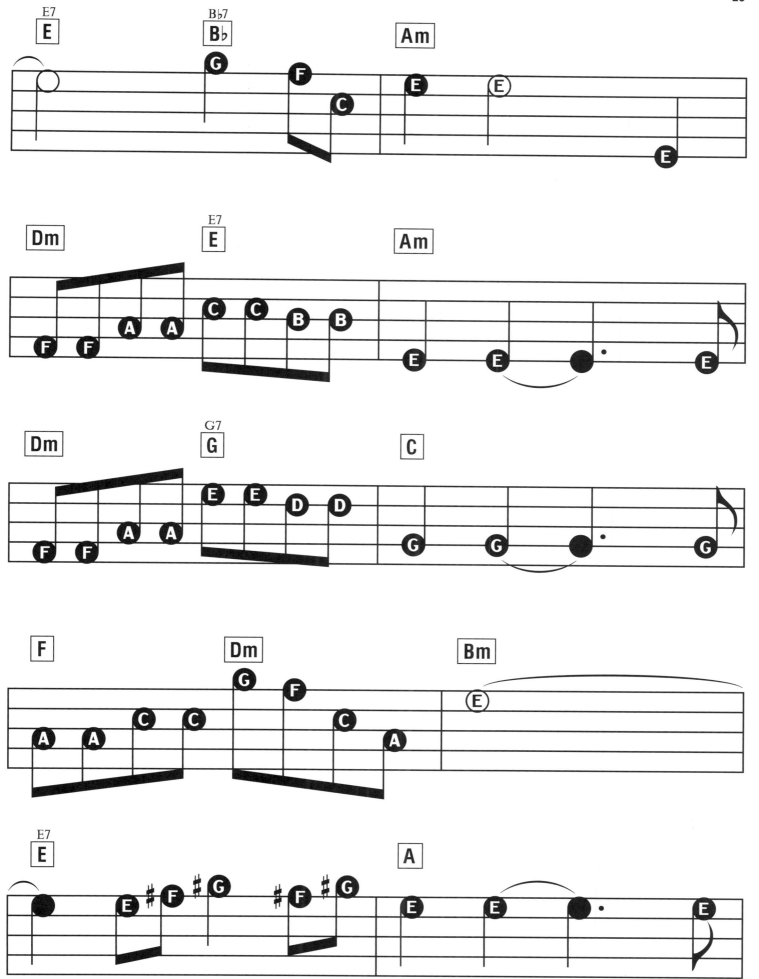

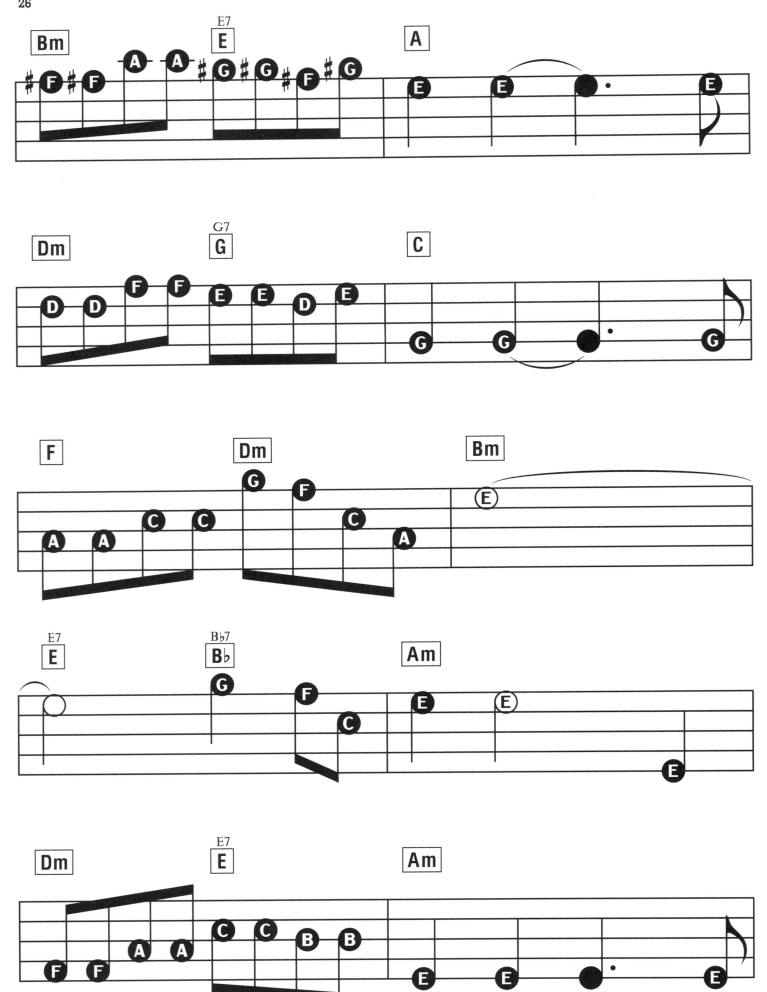

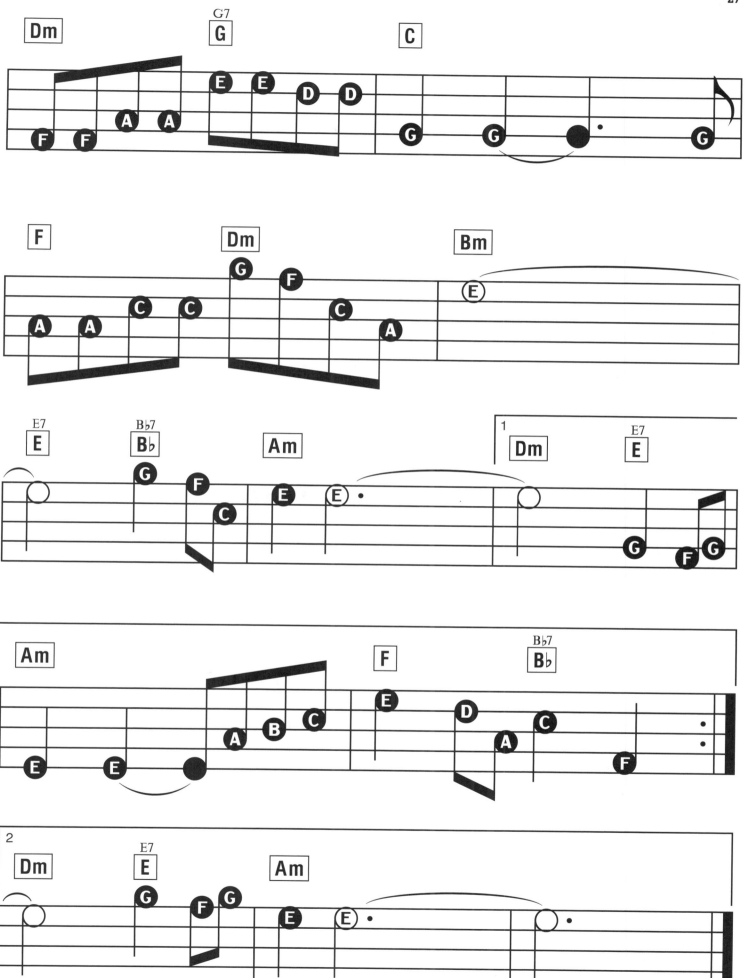

I Mean You

Registration 7
Rhythm: Swing

By Thelonious Monk and
Coleman Hawkins

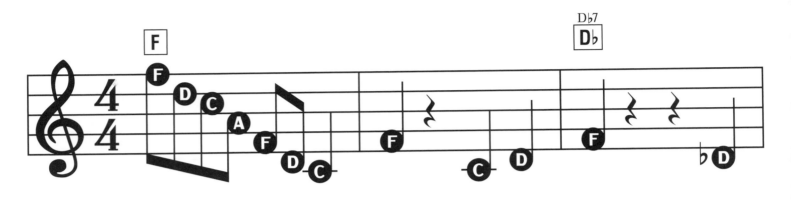

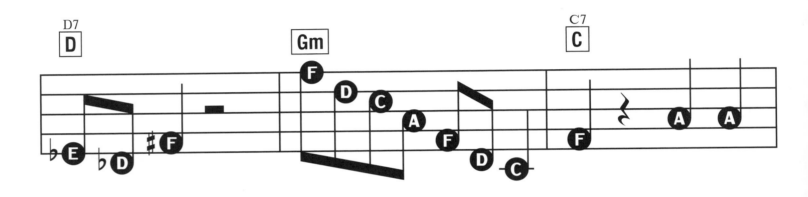

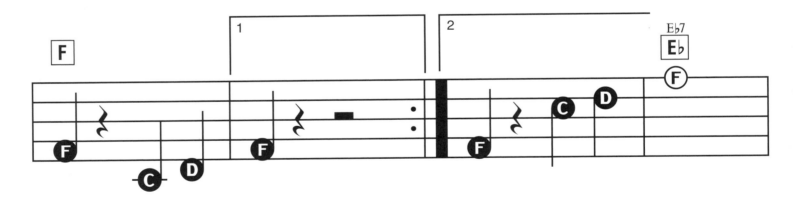

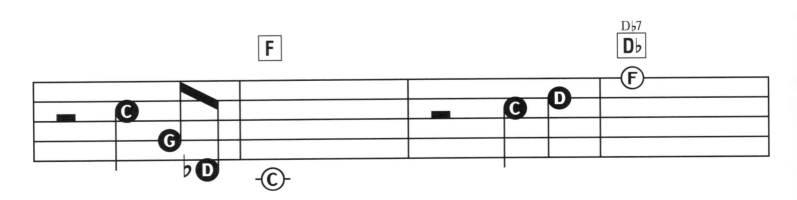

In Walked Bud

Registration 8
Rhythm: Swing

By Thelonious Monk

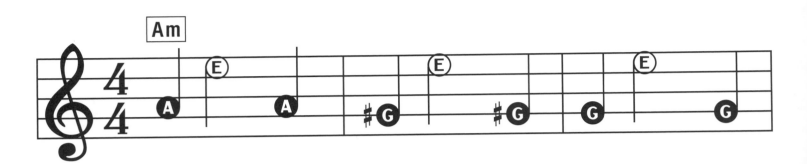

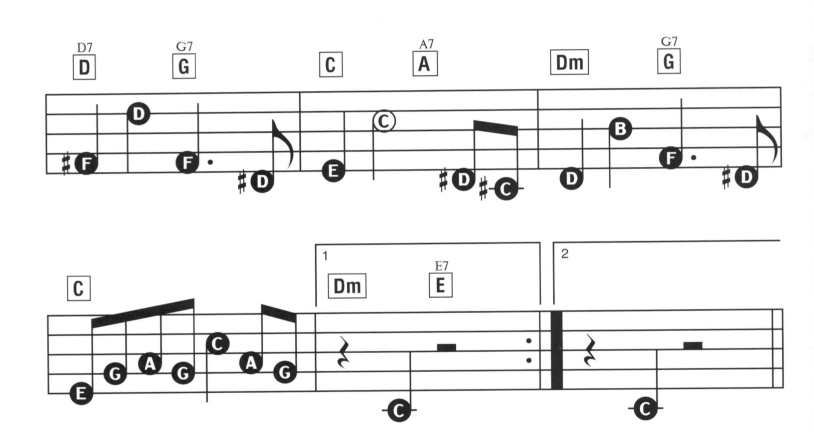

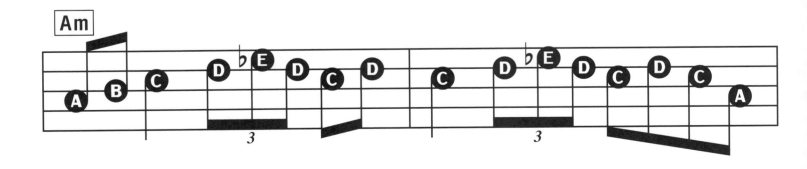

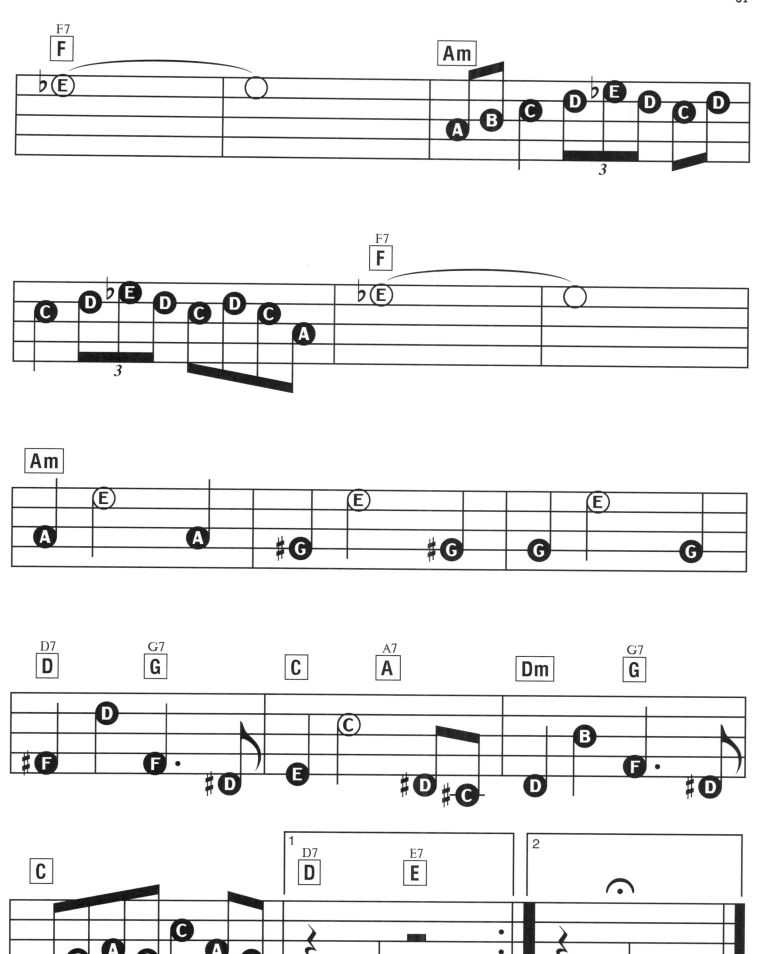

In Your Own Sweet Way

Registration 8
Rhythm: Swing

By Dave Brubeck

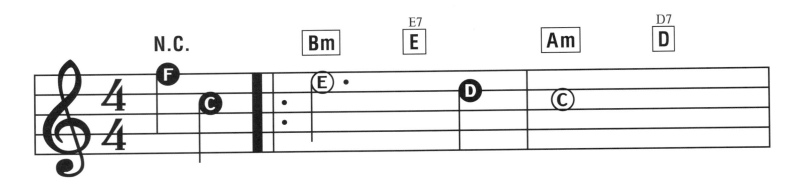

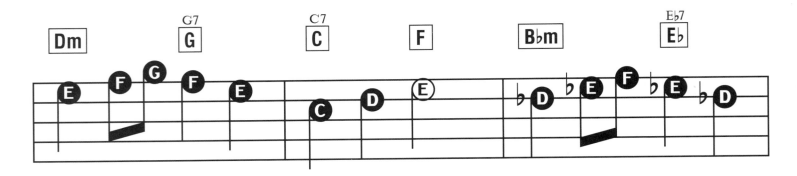

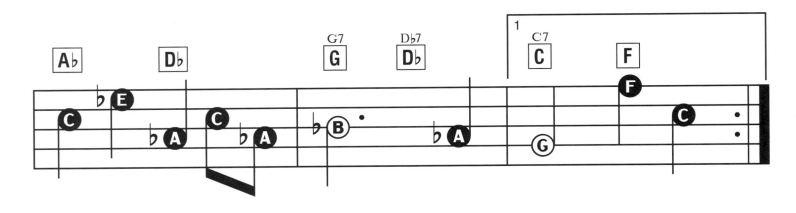

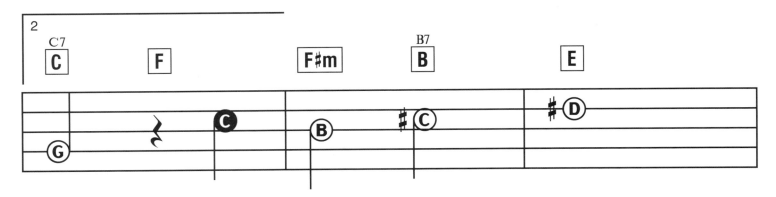

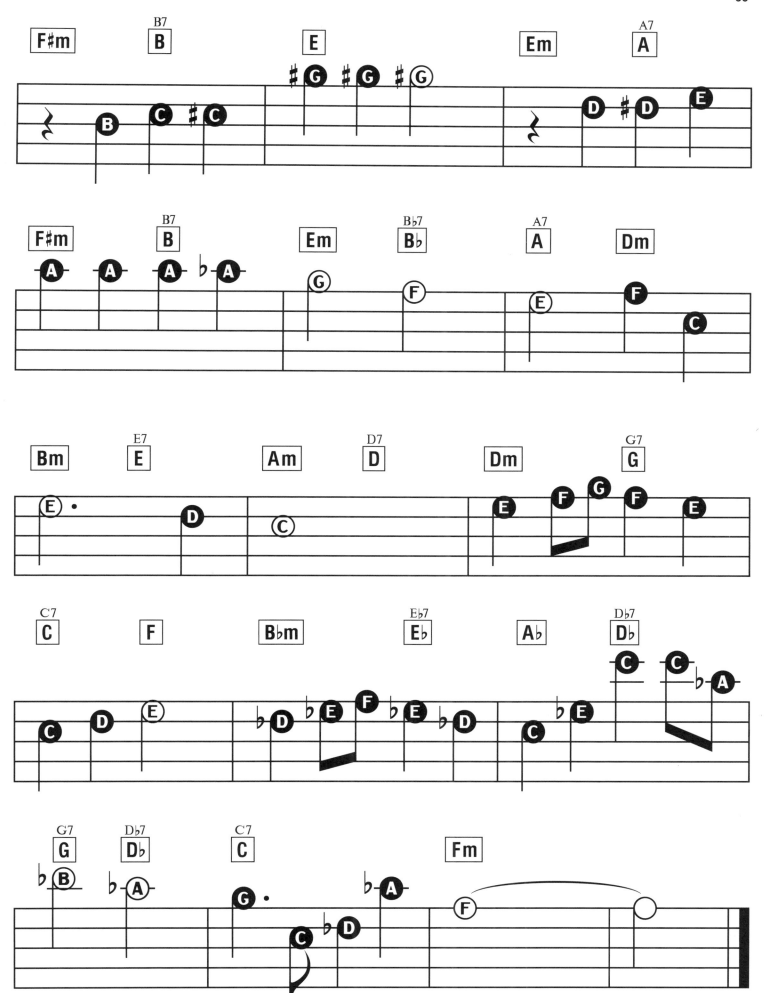

Isfahan
from FAR EAST SUITE

Registration 8
Rhythm: Ballad

By Duke Ellington
and Billy Strayhorn

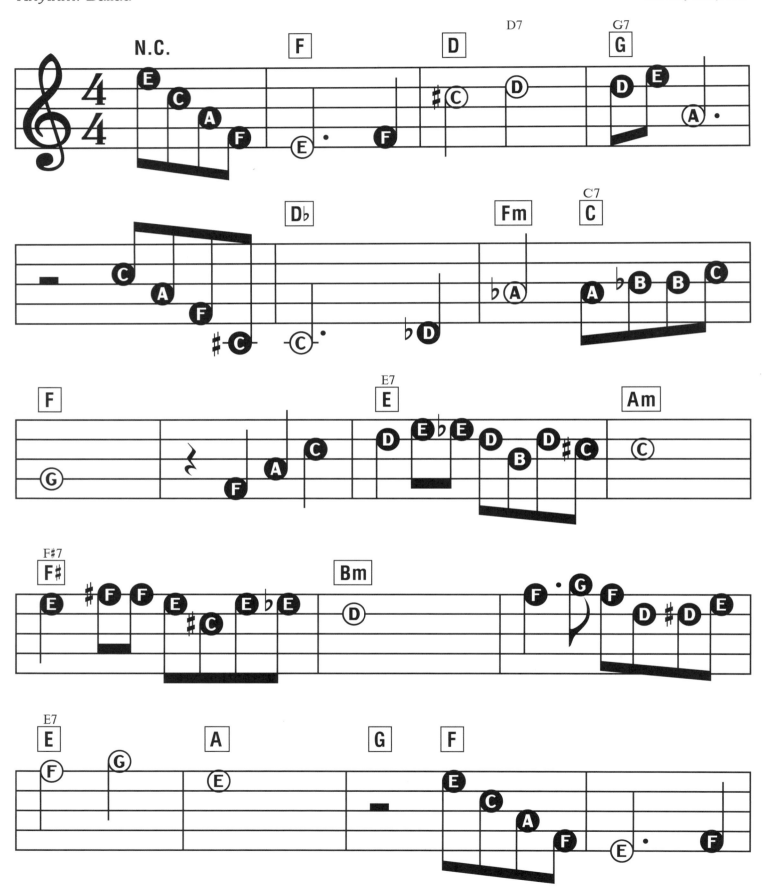

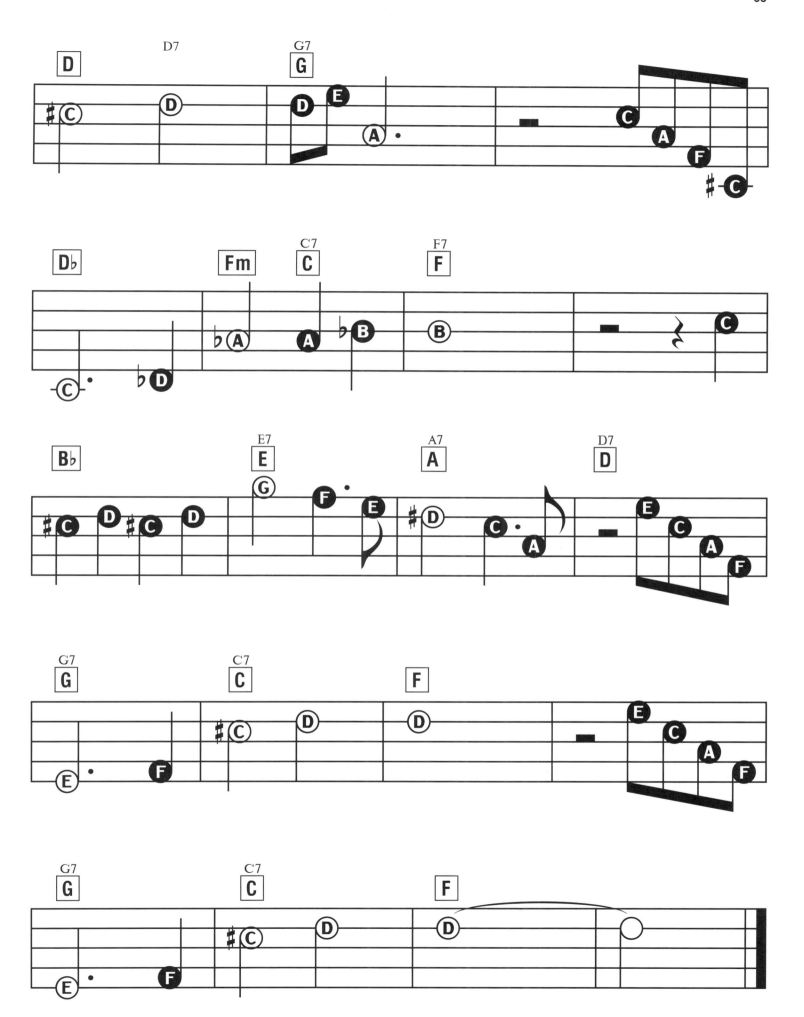

Jordu

Registration 2
Rhythm: Swing

By Duke Jordan

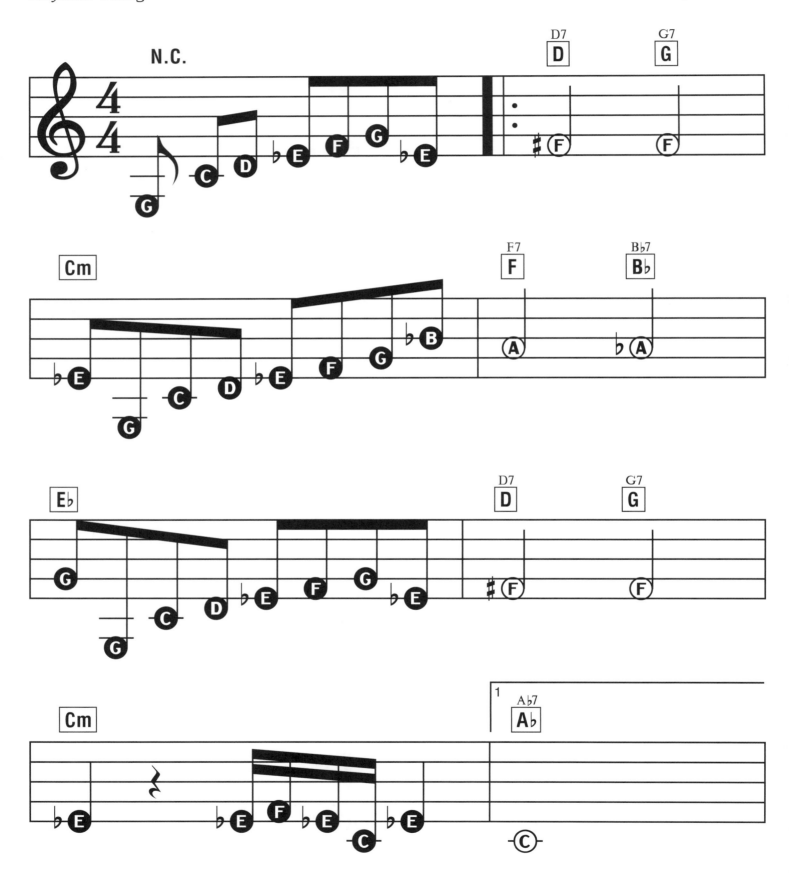

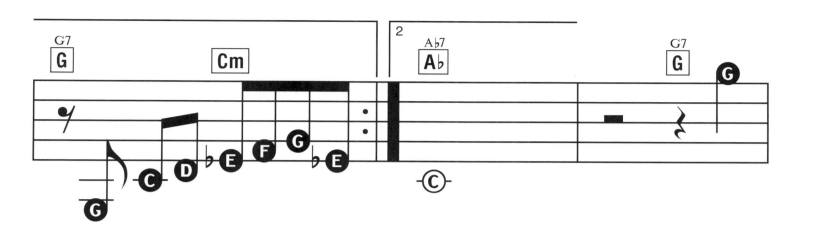

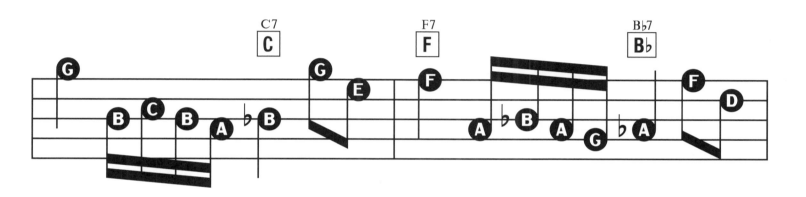

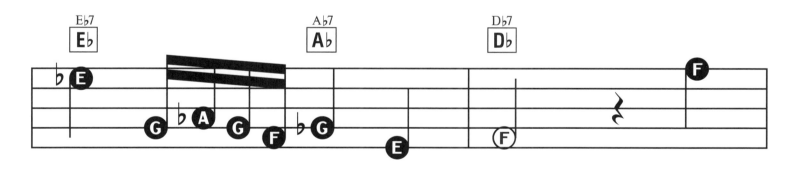

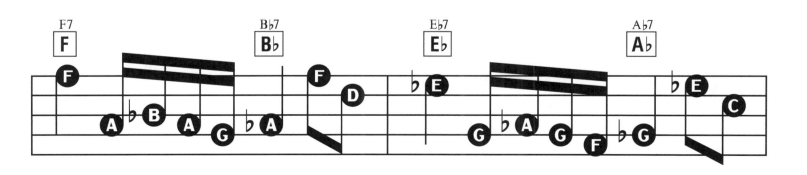

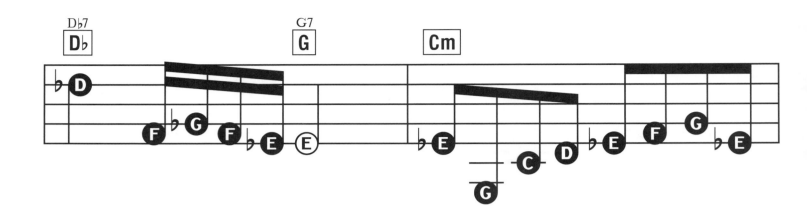

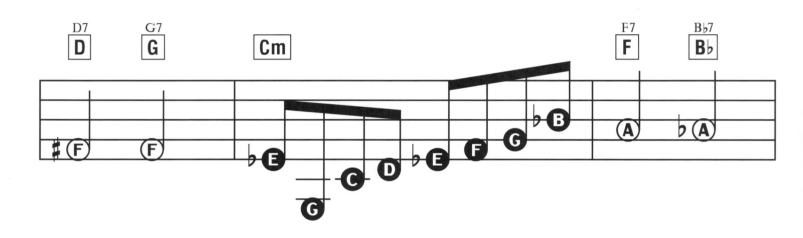

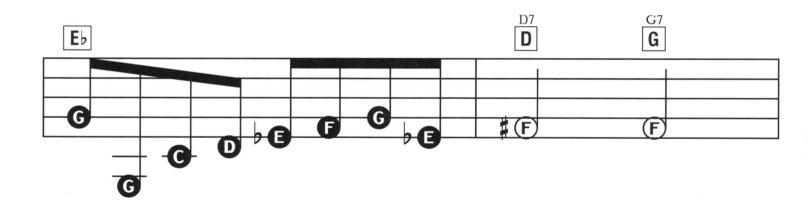

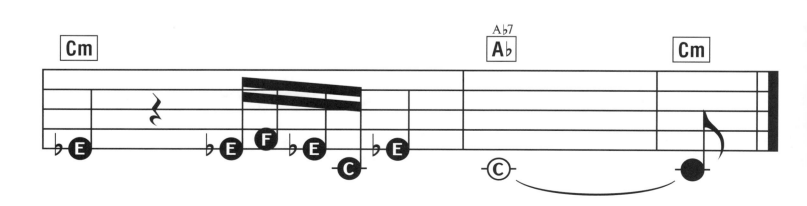

La Ronde

Registration 5
Rhythm: Swing

By John Lewis

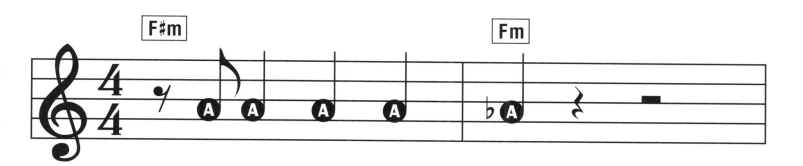

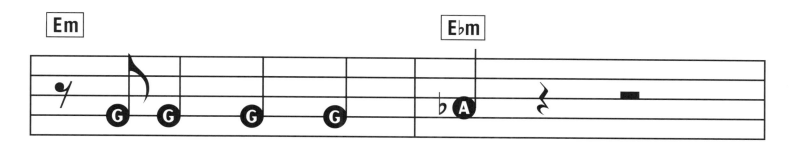

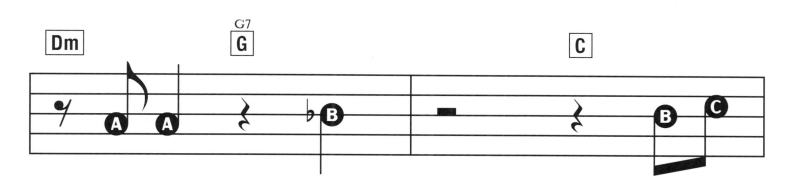

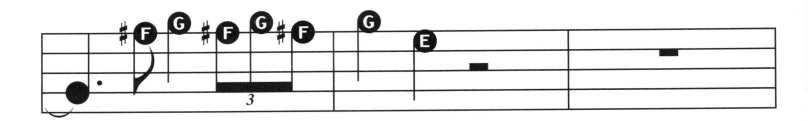

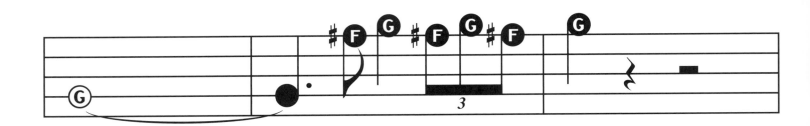

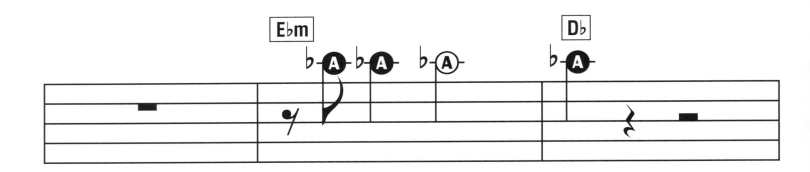

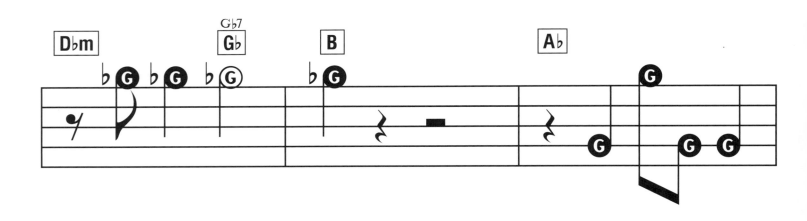

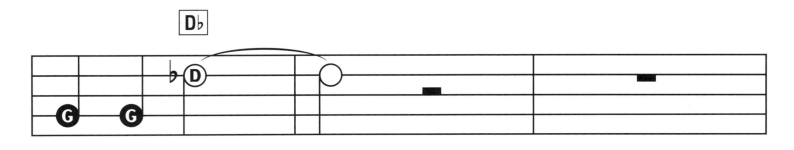

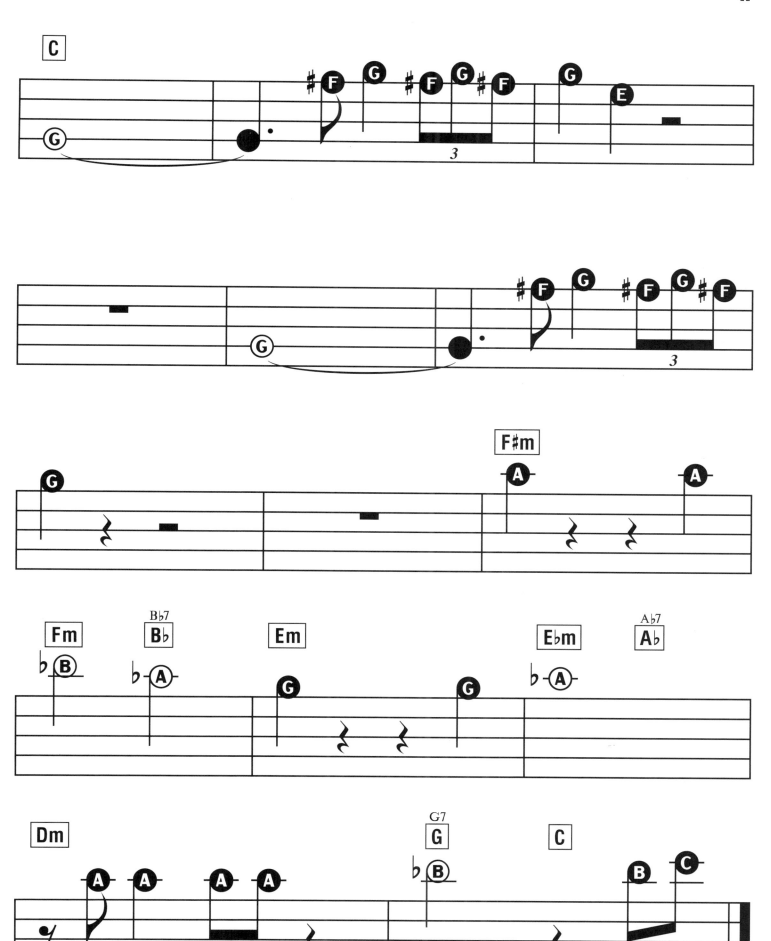

Jump for Joy

Registration 2
Rhythm: Swing

By Duke Ellington, Paul Webster
and Sid Kuller

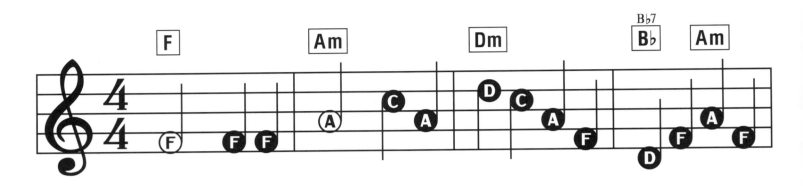

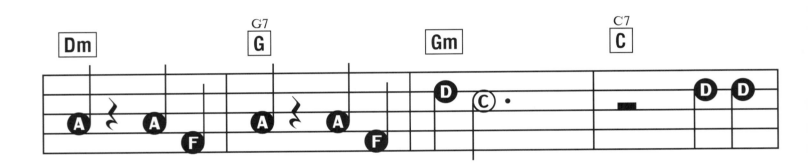

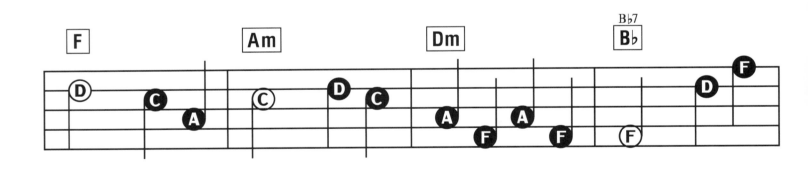

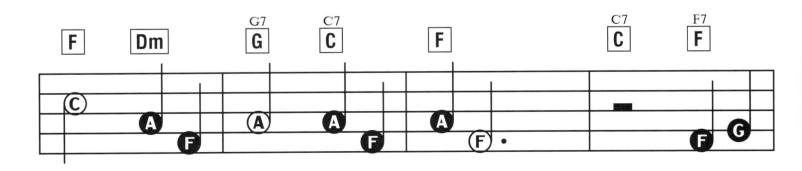

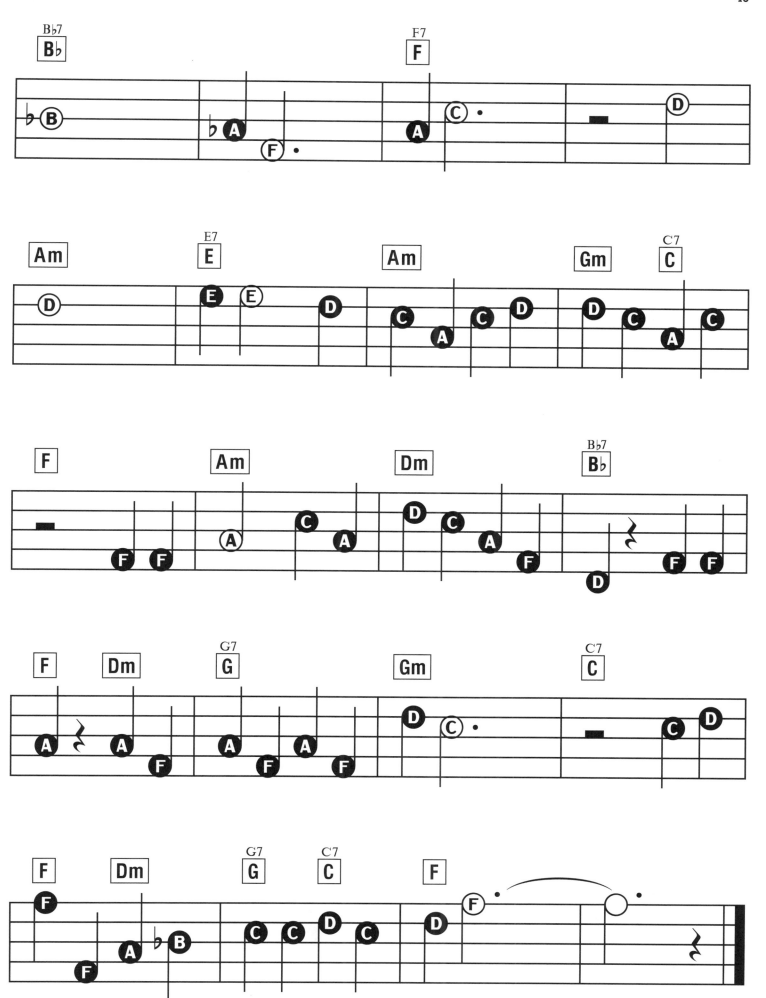

Just the Two of Us

Registration 4
Rhythm: Latin

Words and Music by Ralph MacDonald,
William Salter and Bill Withers

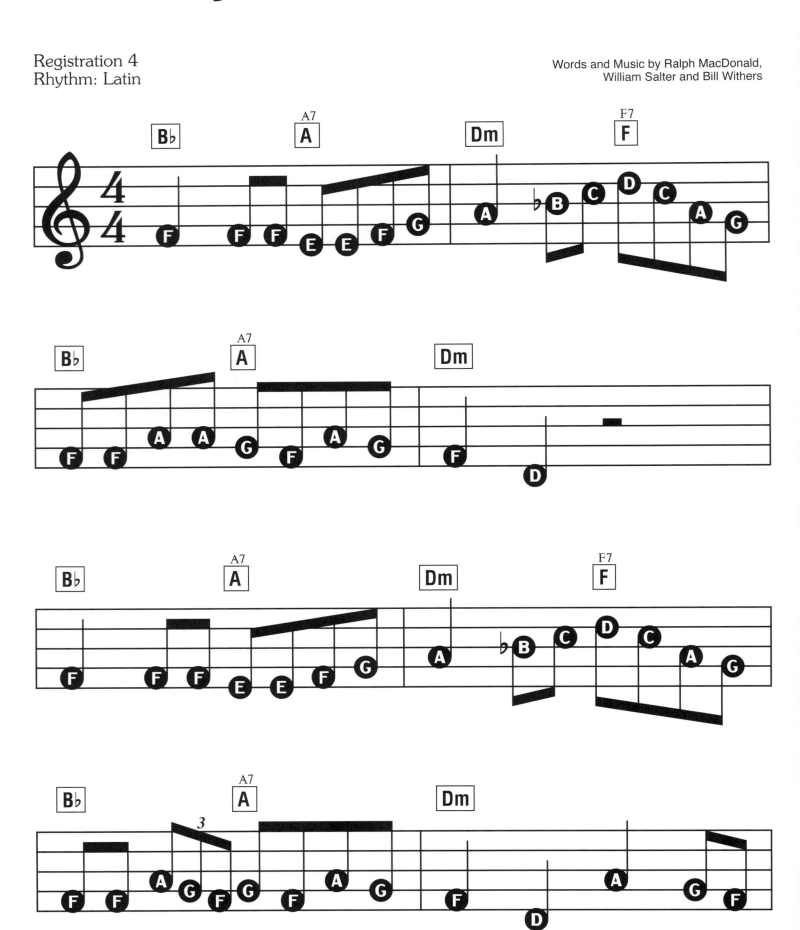

45

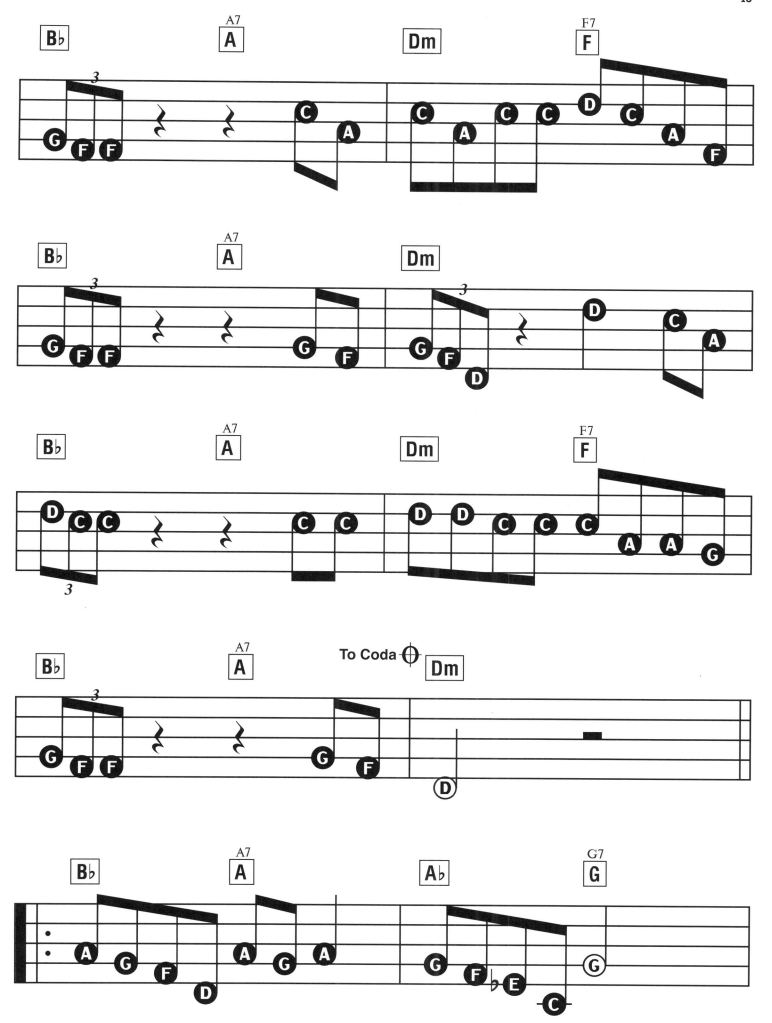

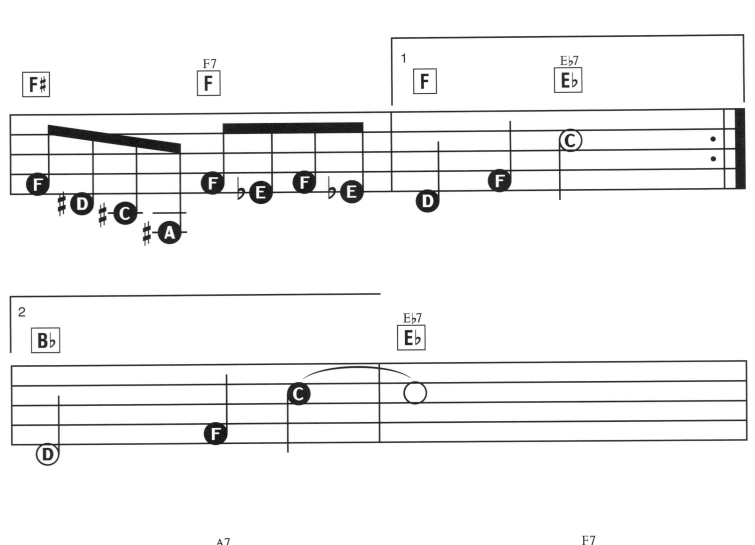

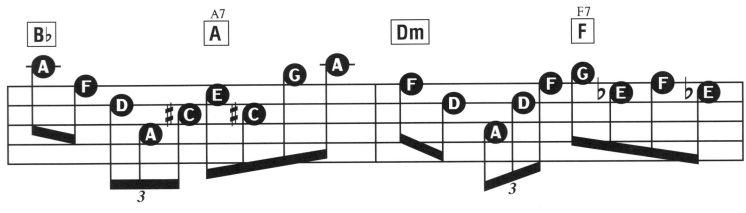

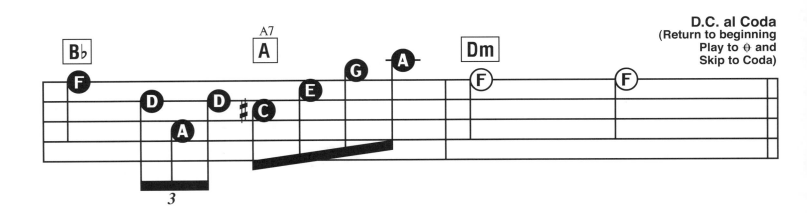

D.C. al Coda
(Return to beginning
Play to ⊕ and
Skip to Coda)

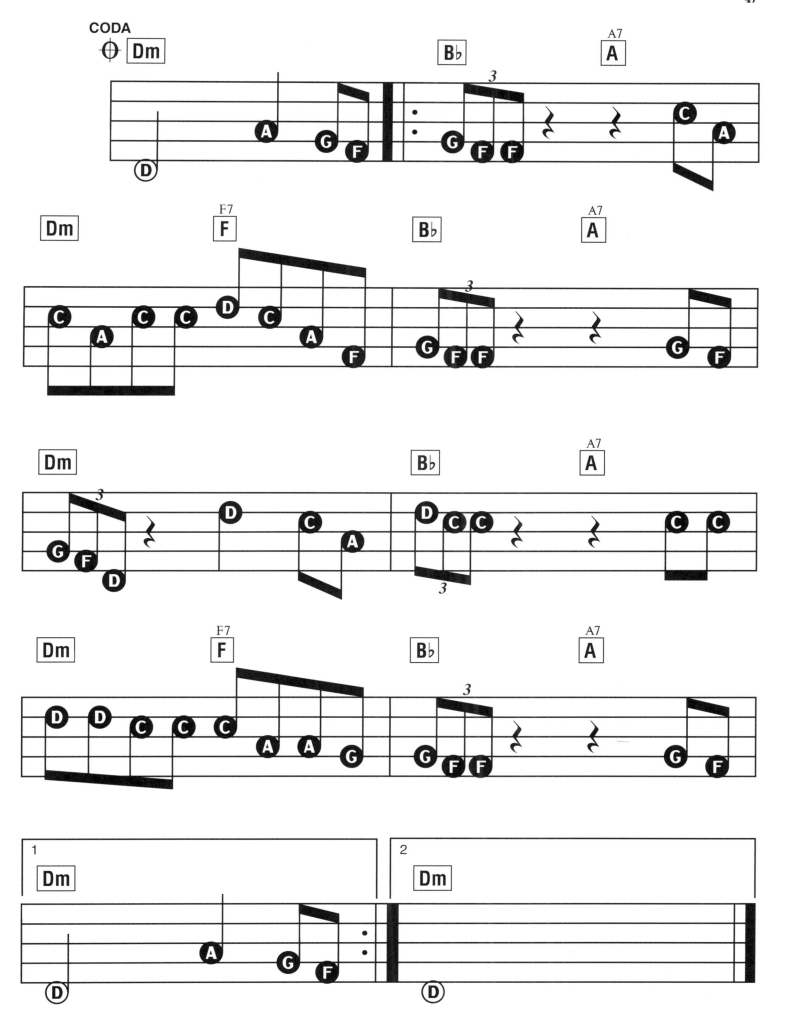

Killer Joe

Registration 7
Rhythm: Swing

By Benny Golson

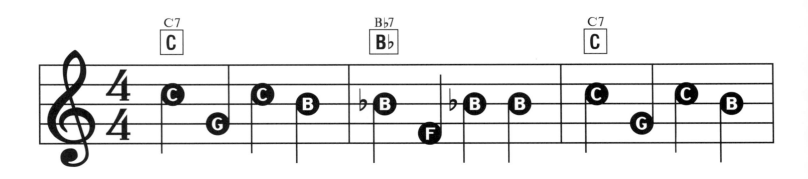

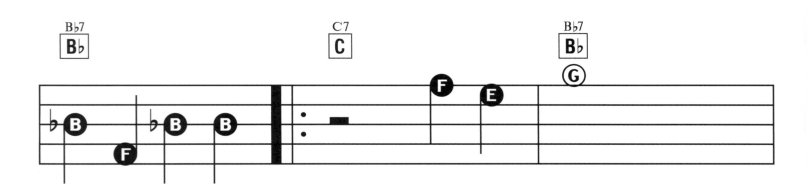

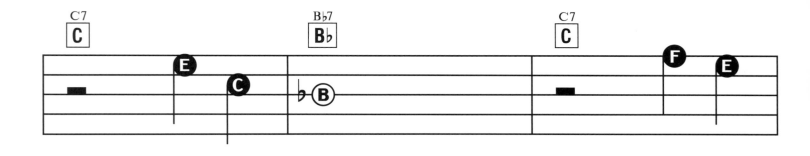

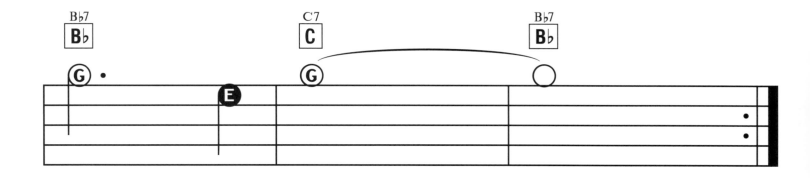

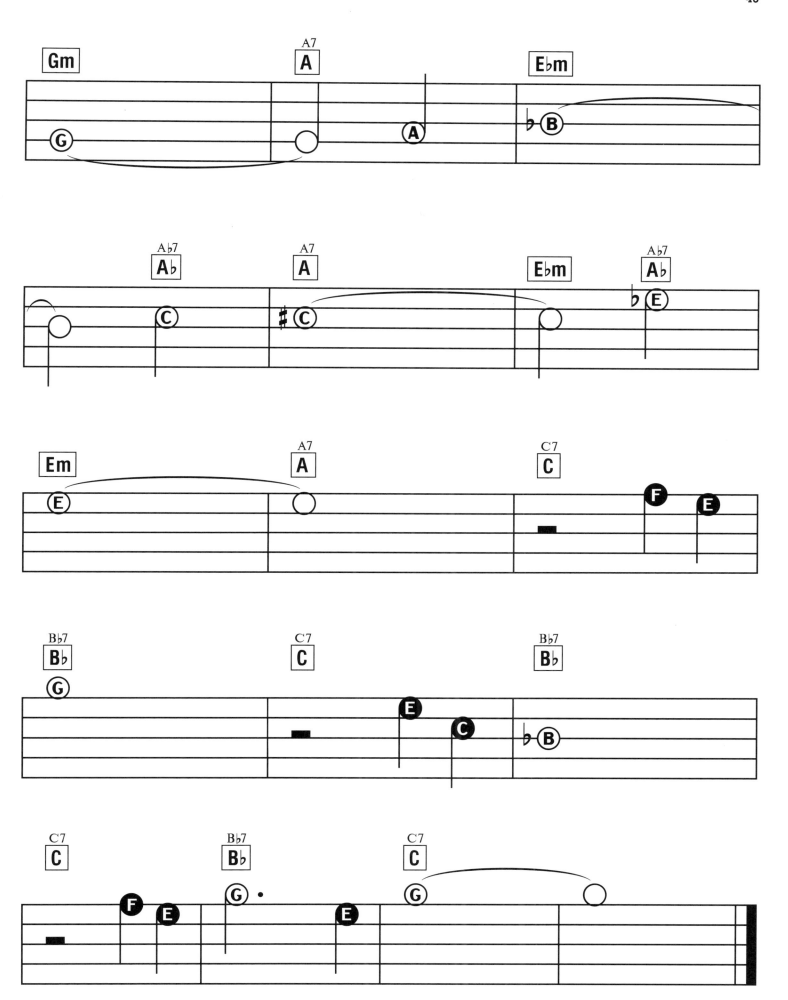

Lady Sings the Blues

Registration 7
Rhythm: Swing

Words and Music by Herbert Nichols
and Billie Holiday

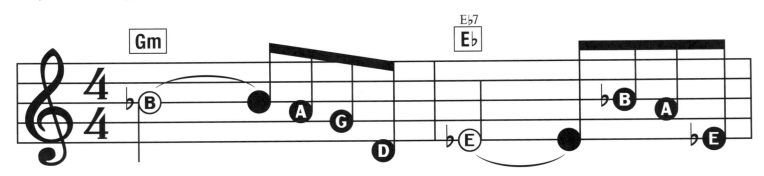

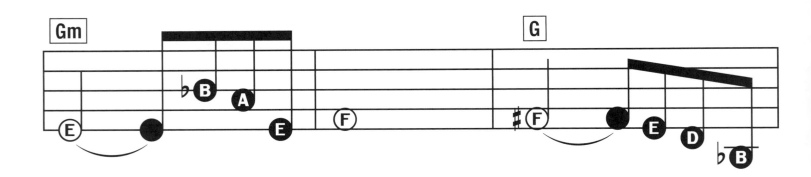

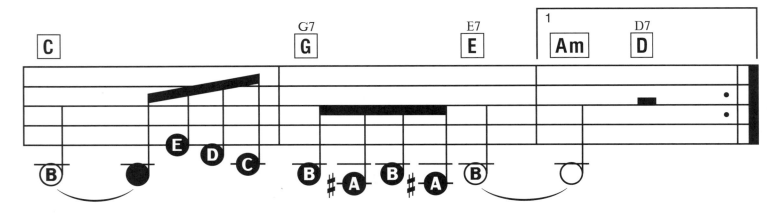

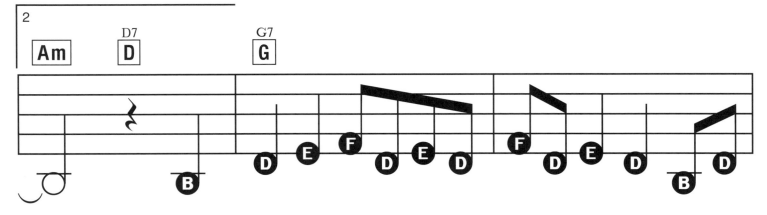

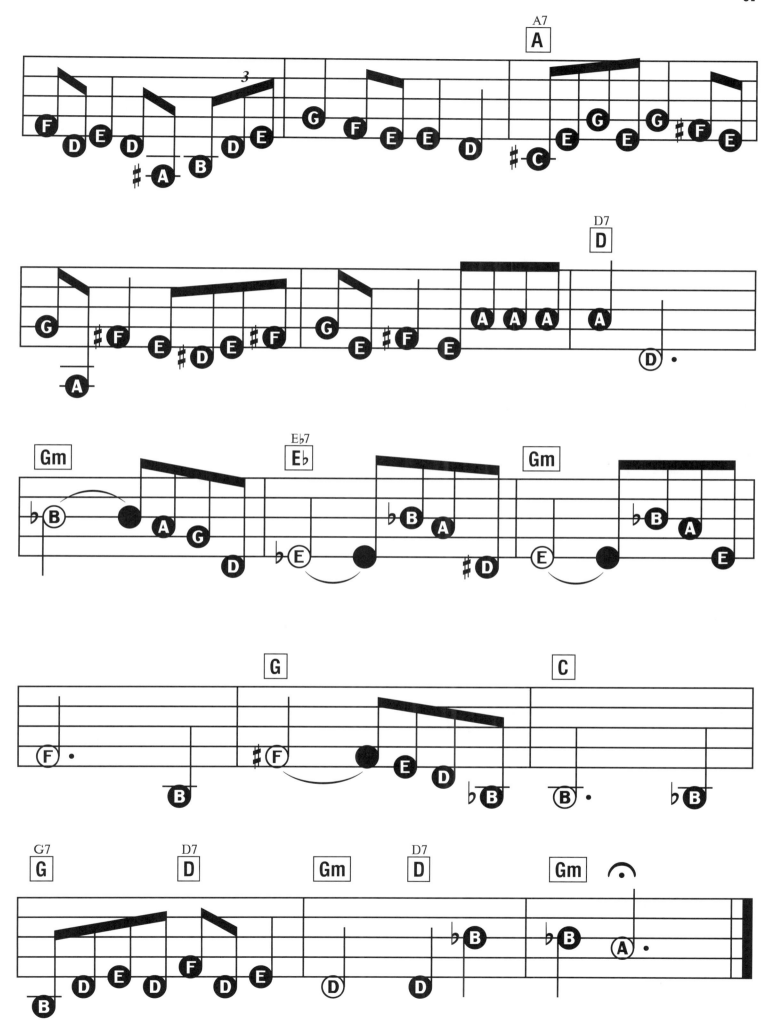

Line for Lyons

Registration 7
Rhythm: Swing

By Gerry Mulligan

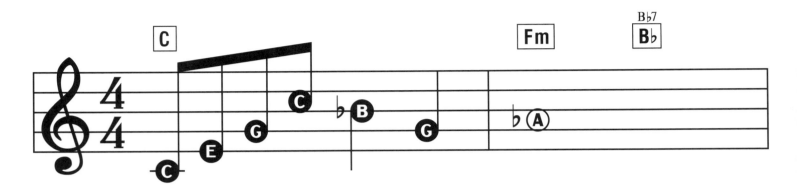

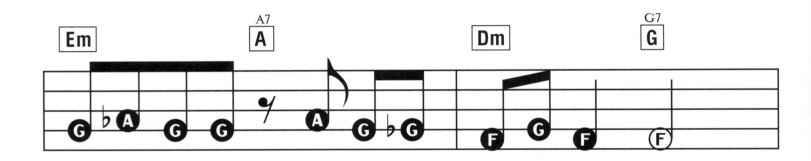

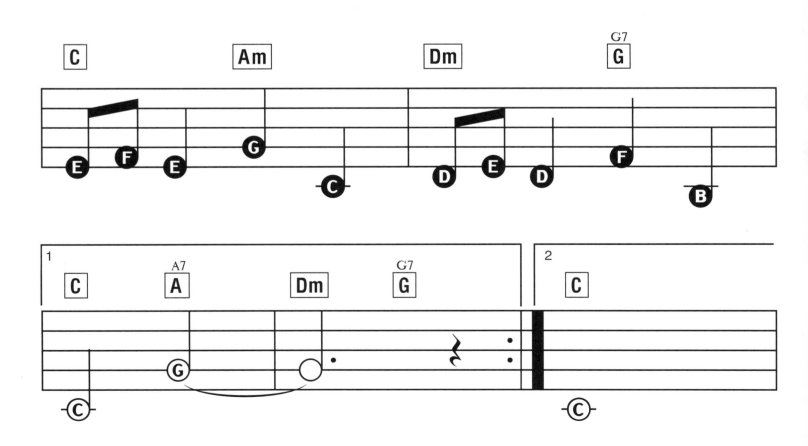

53

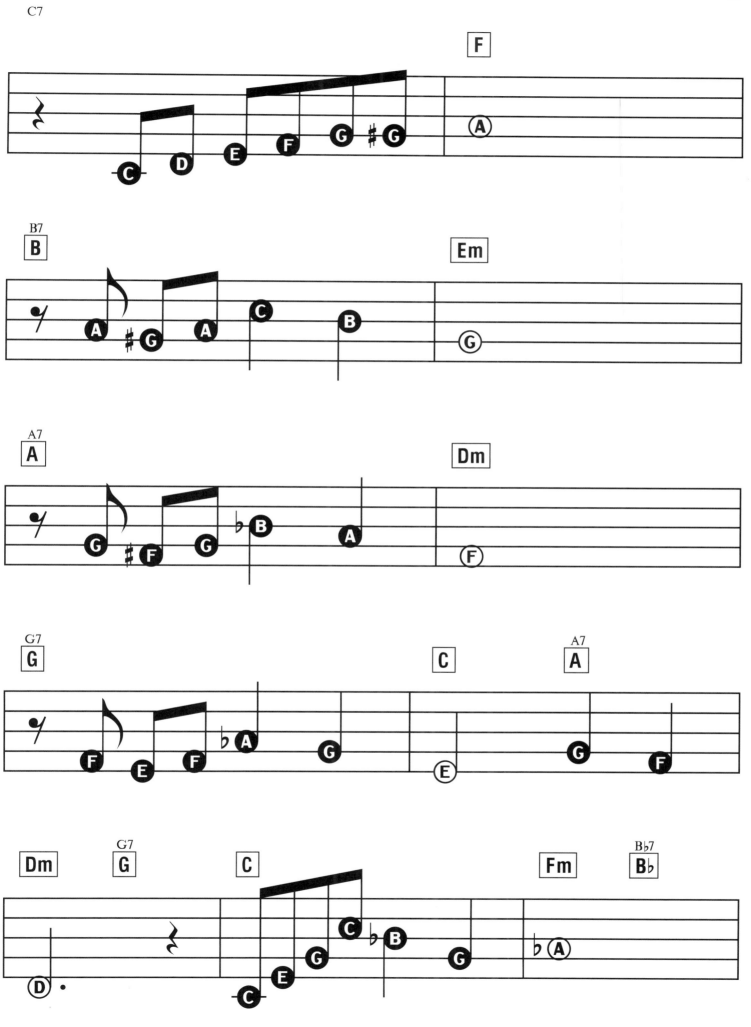

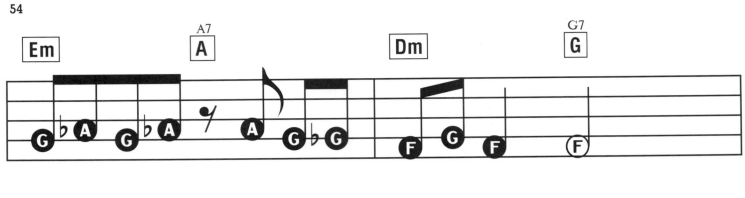

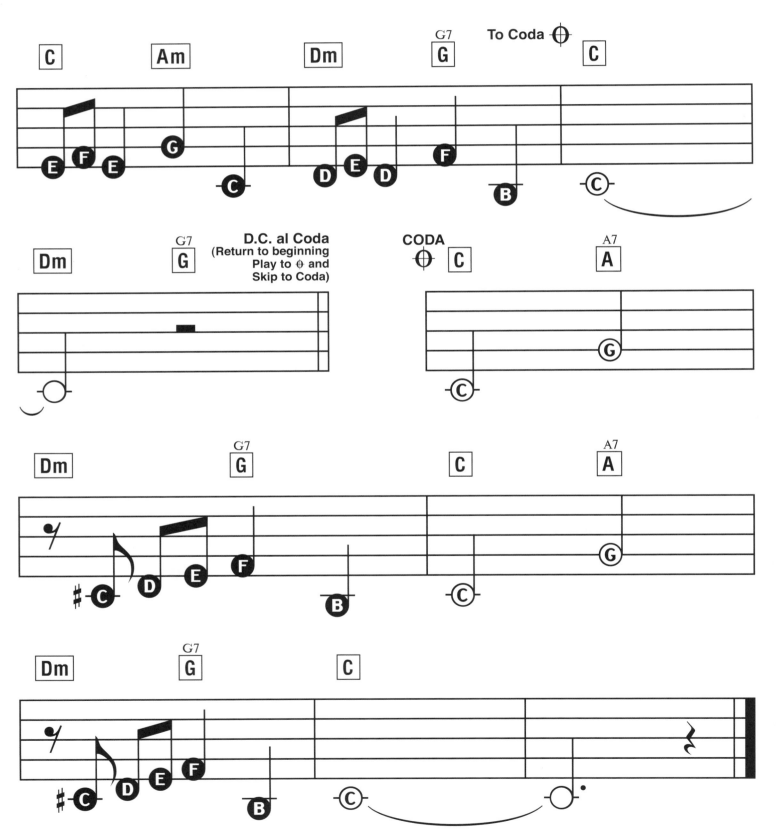

Manteca

Registration 7
Rhythm: Latin

By Dizzy Gillespie, Walter Gil Fuller
and Luciano Pozo Gonzales

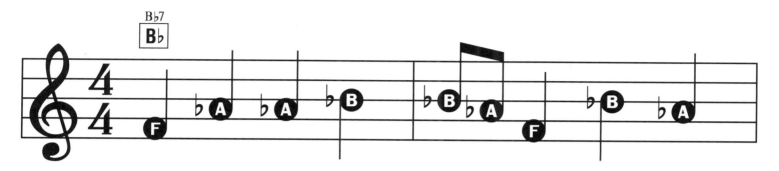

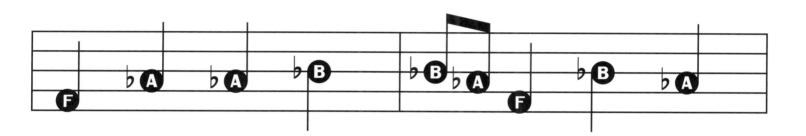

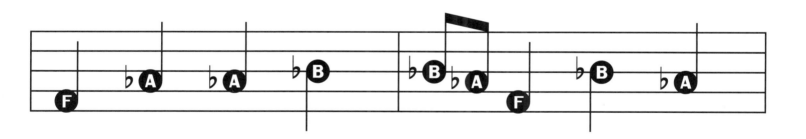

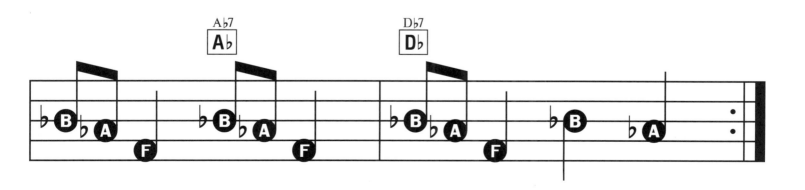

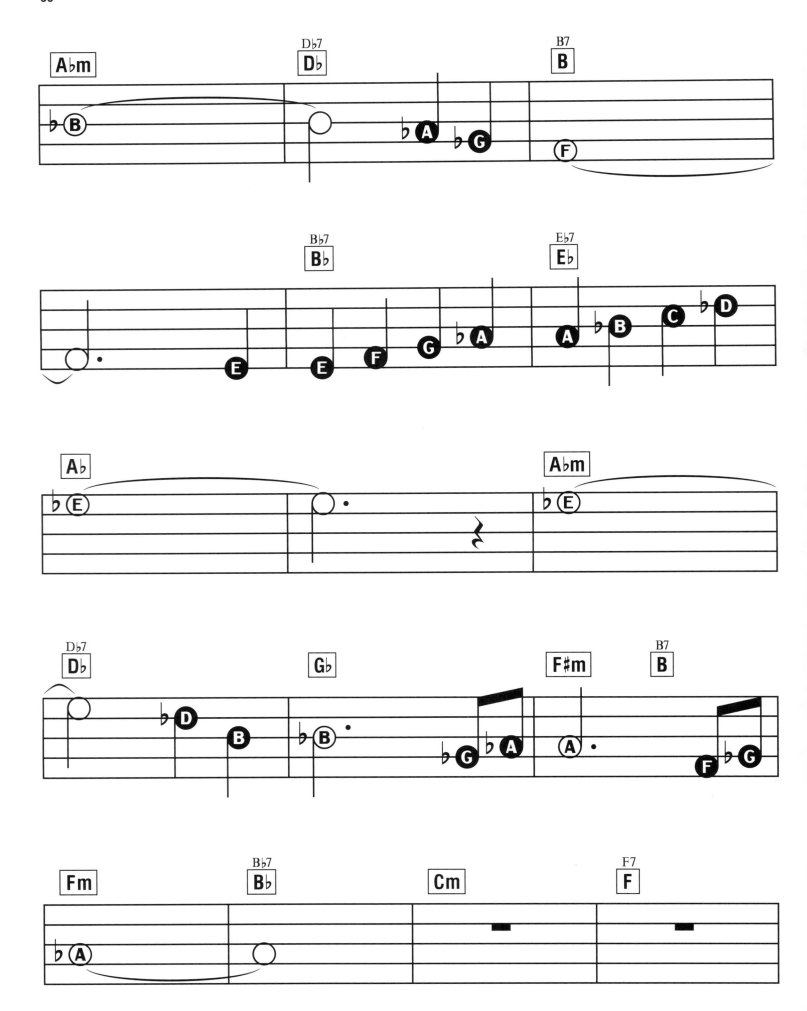

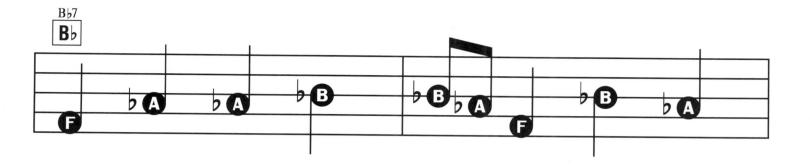

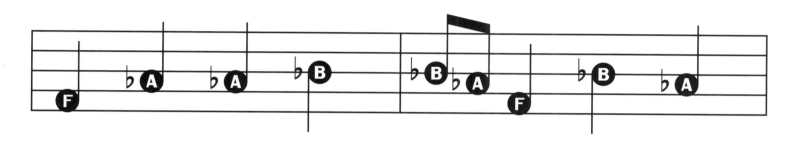

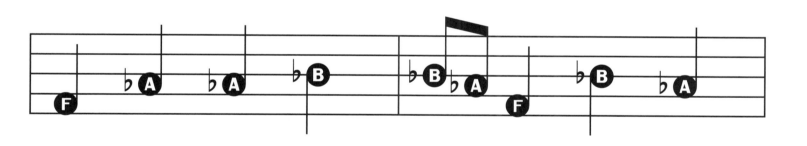

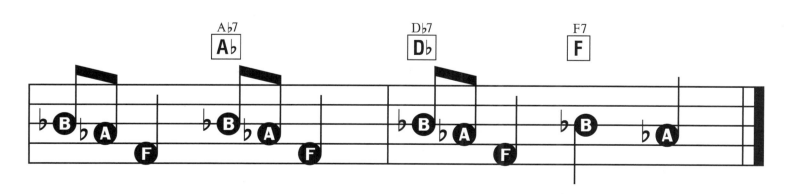

Mercy, Mercy, Mercy

Registration 2
Rhythm: Swing

Composed by Josef Zawinul

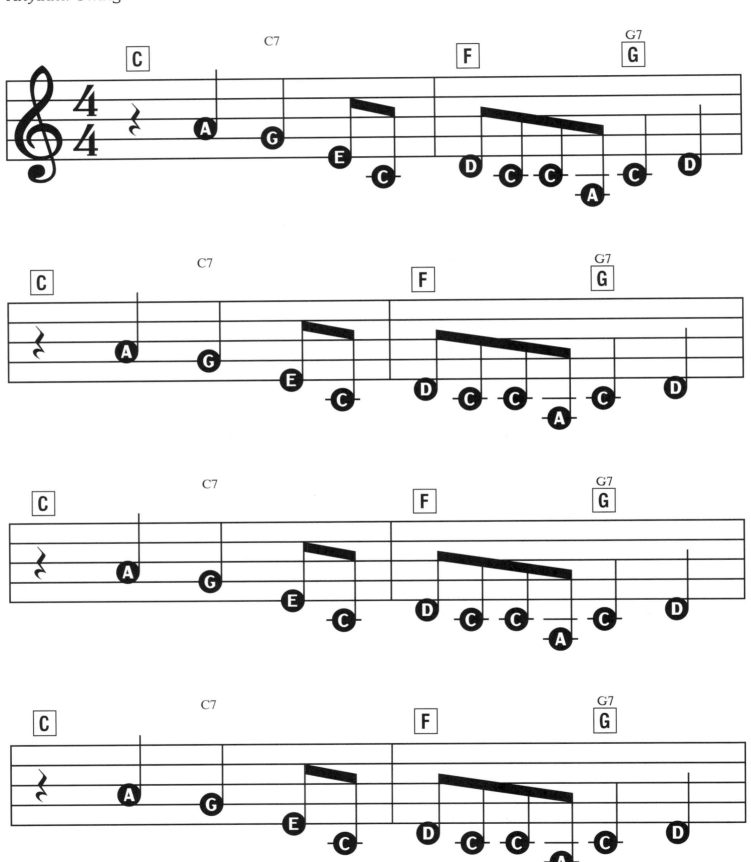

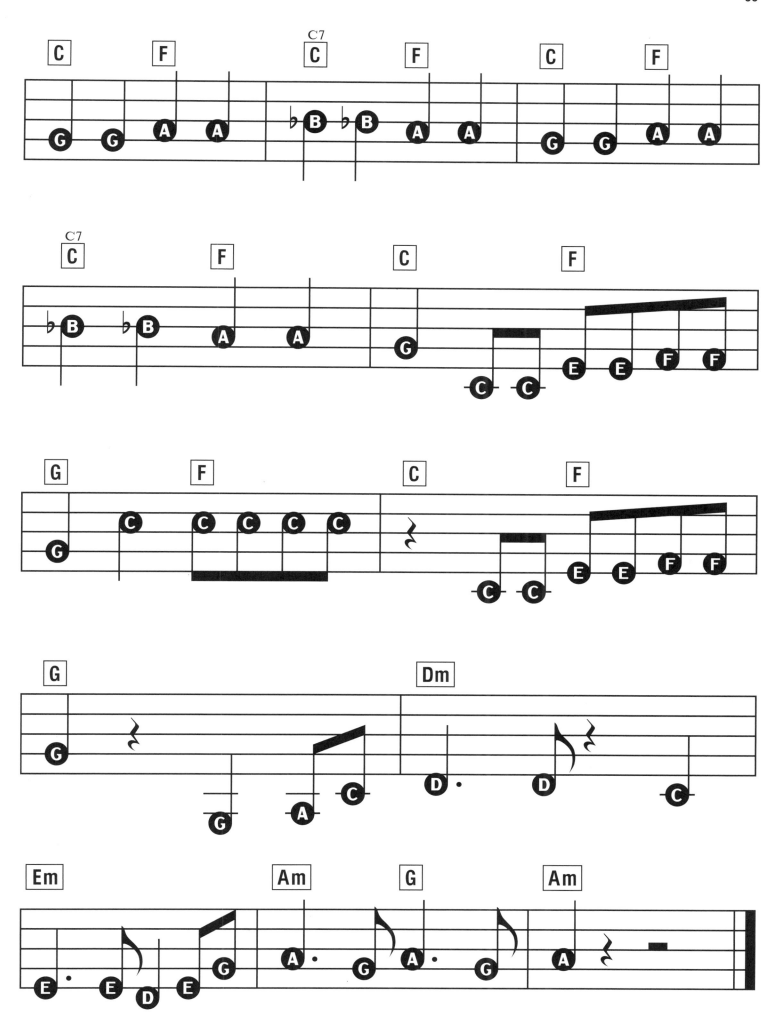

Morning Dance

Registration 4
Rhythm: Latin or Samba

By Jay Beckenstein

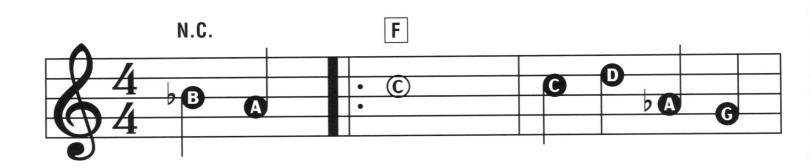

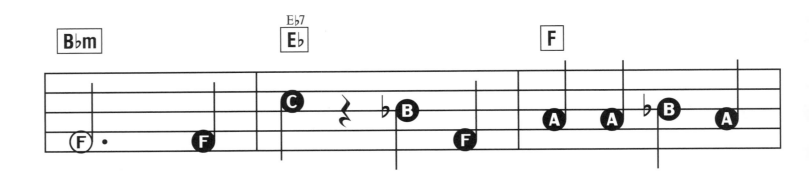

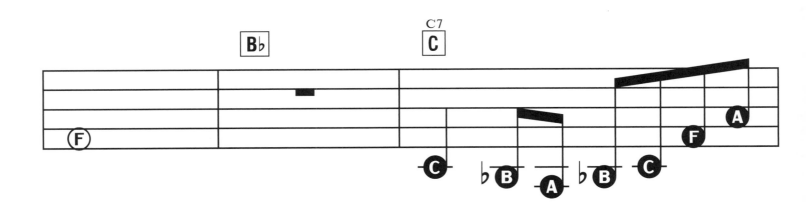

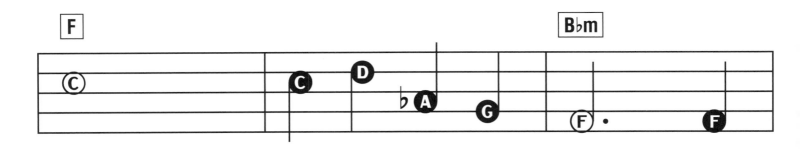

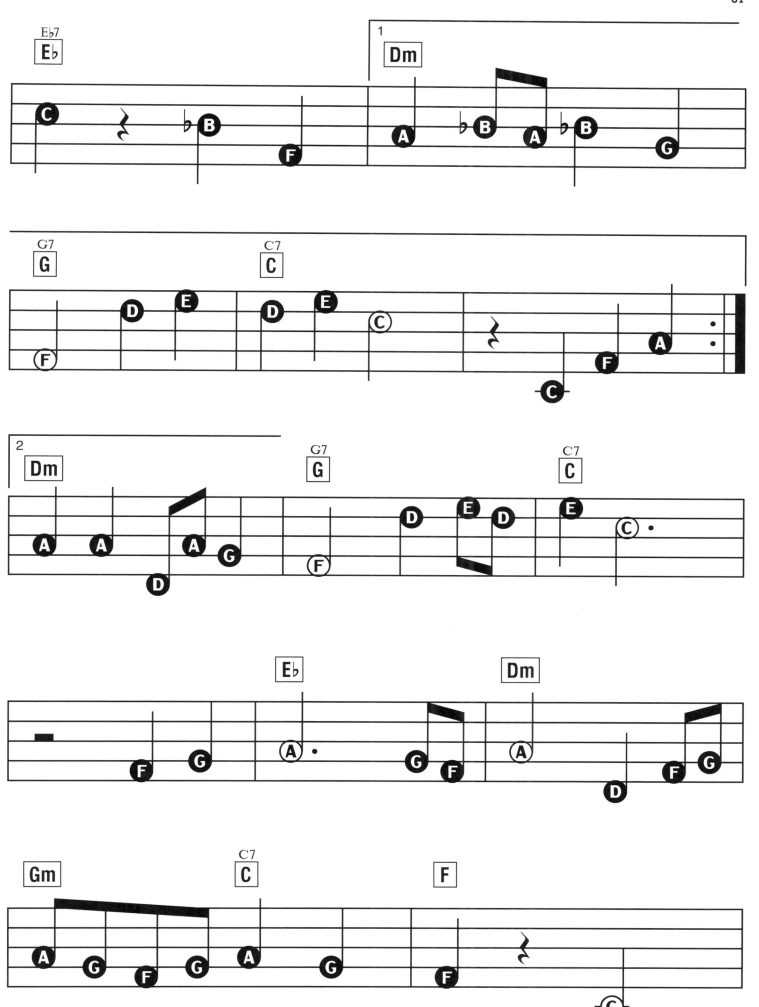

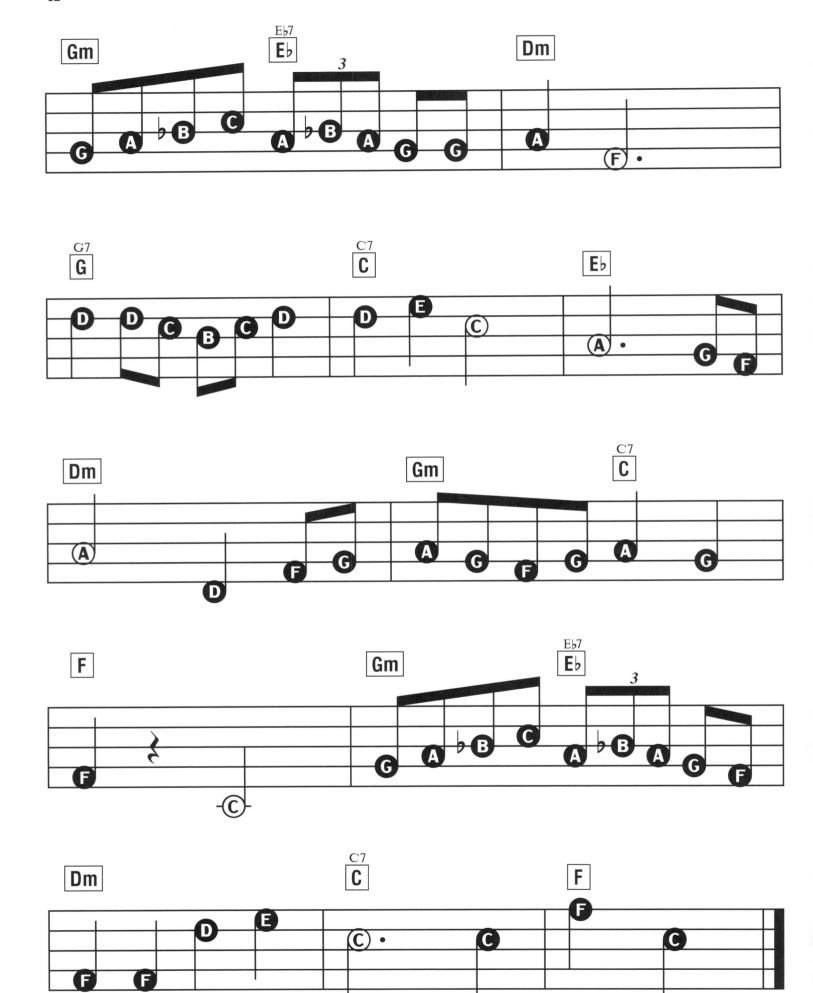

Nica's Dream

Registration 8
Rhythm: Latin

Words and Music by
Horace Silver

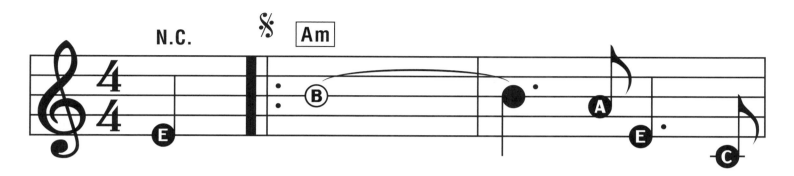

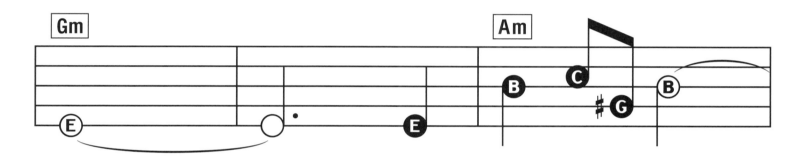

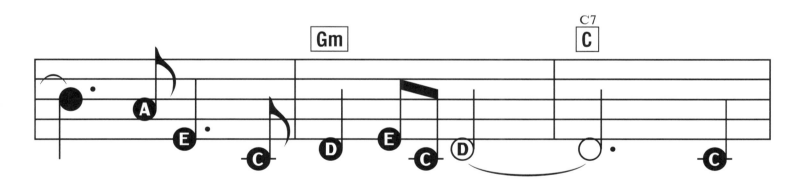

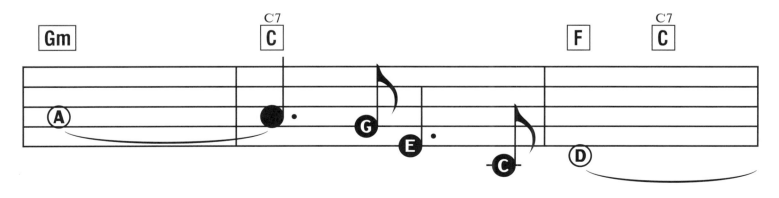

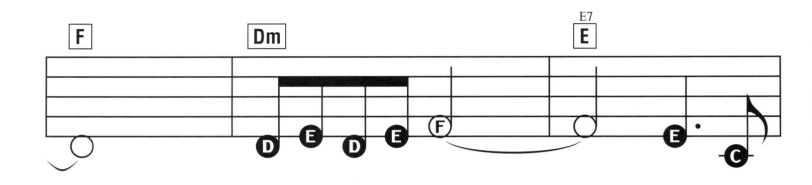

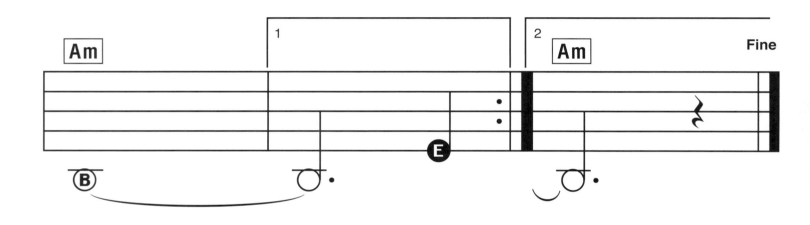

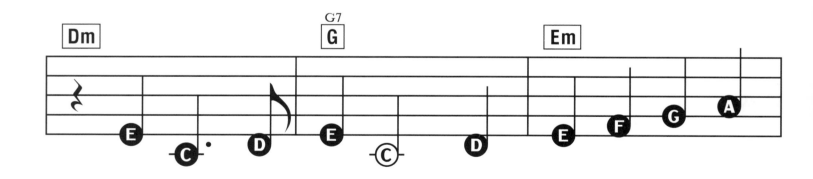

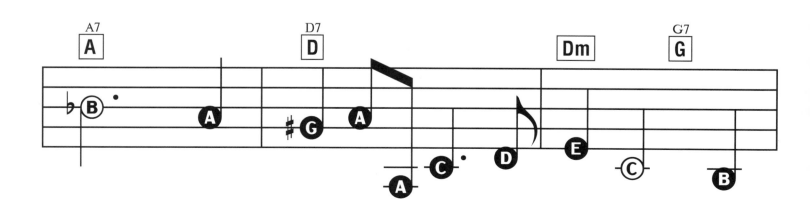

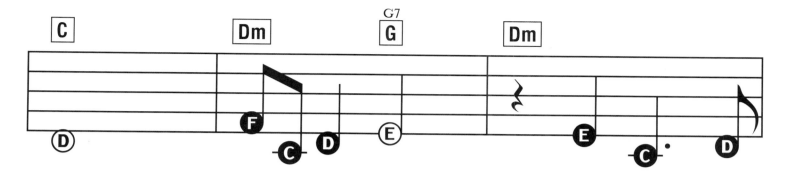

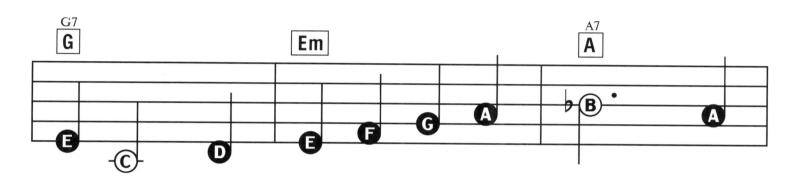

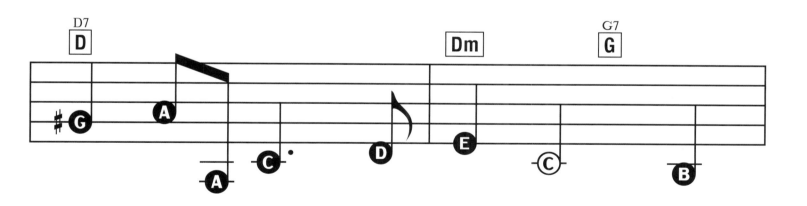

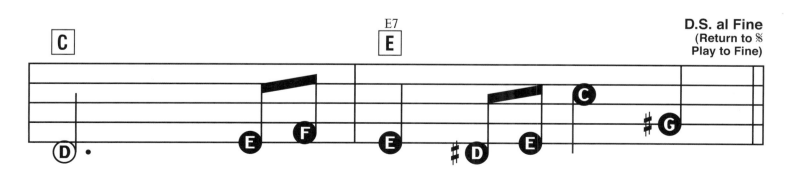

Moten Swing

Registration 3
Rhythm: Swing

By Buster Moten
and Bennie Moten

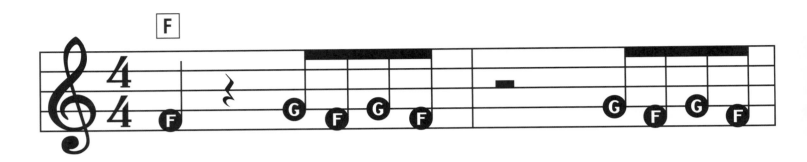

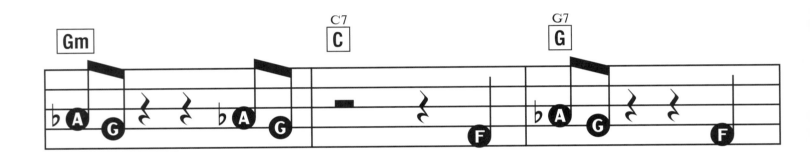

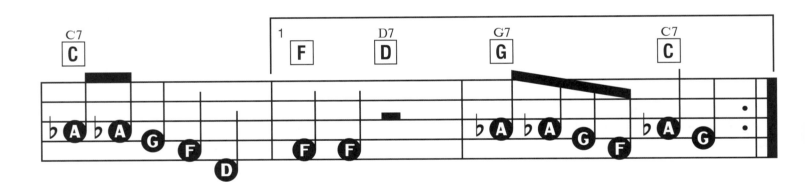

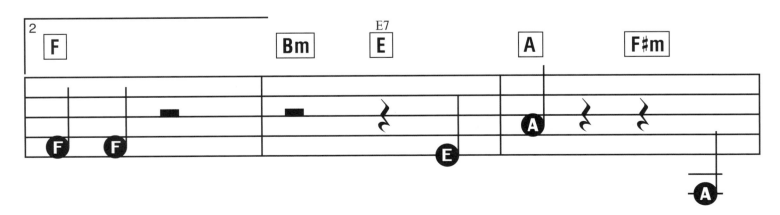

67

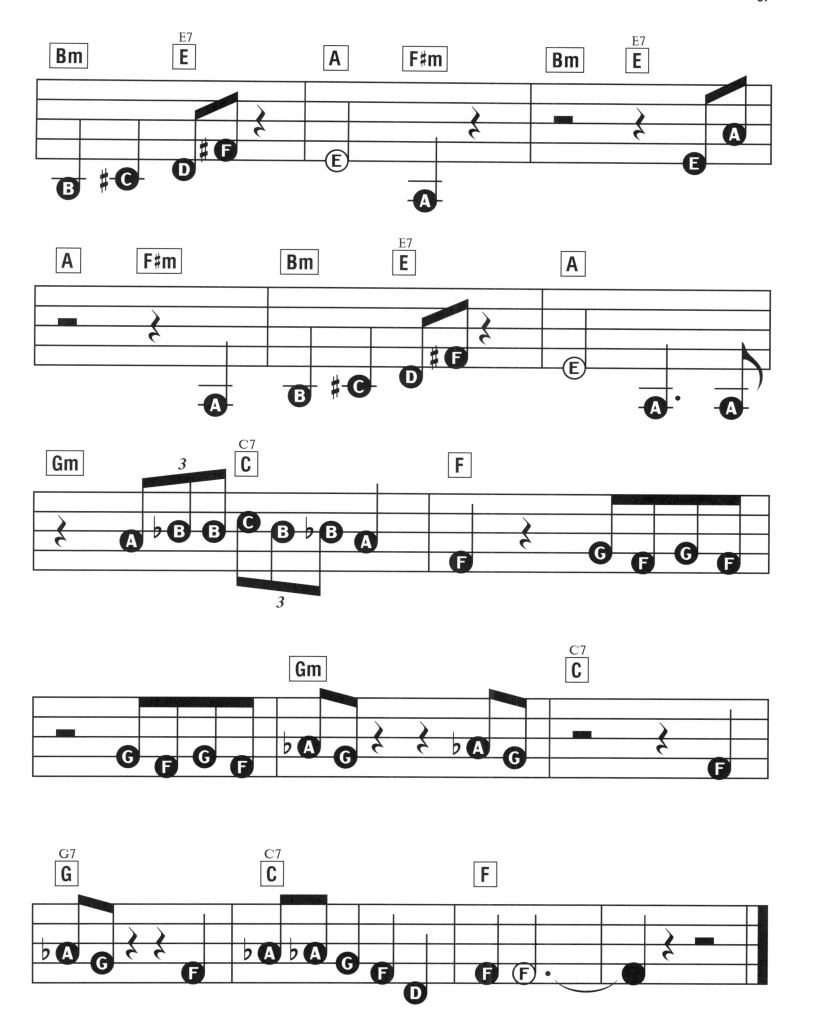

A Night in Tunisia

Registration 7
Rhythm: Swing or Shuffle

By John "Dizzy" Gillespie
and Frank Paparelli

Nuages

Registration 2
Rhythm: Ballad or Swing

By Django Reinhardt
and Jacques Larue

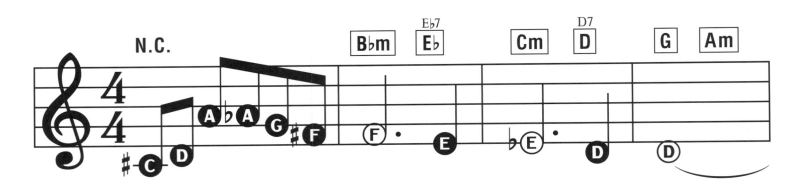

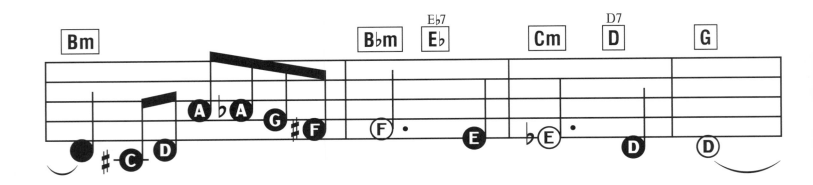

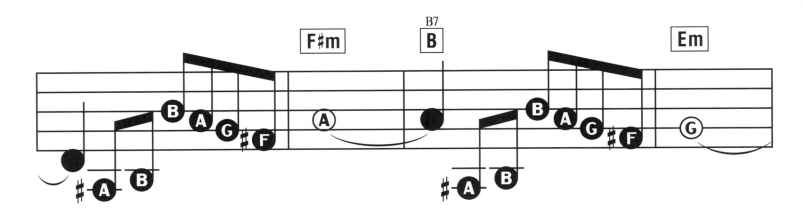

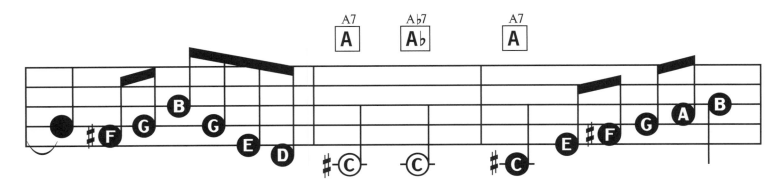

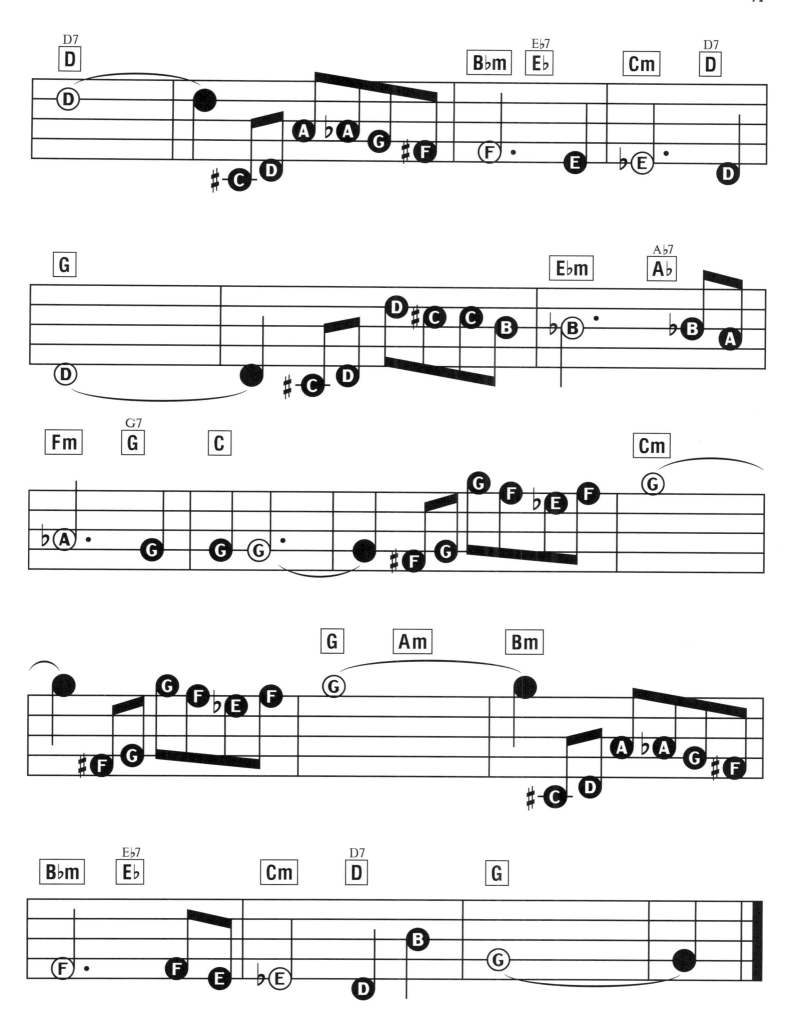

Operator

Registration 4
Rhythm: Swing

Words and Music by
William Spivery

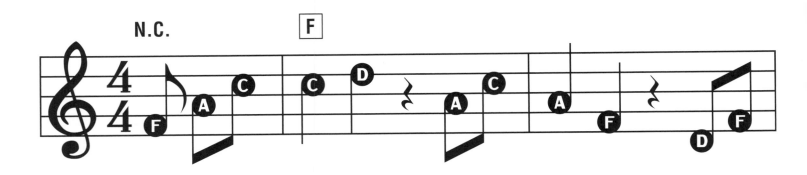

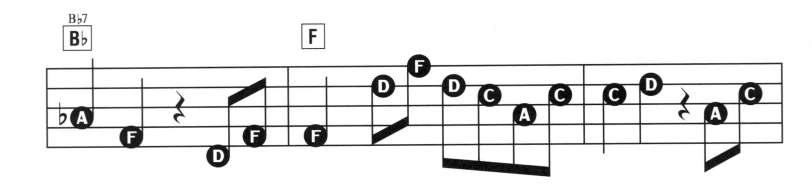

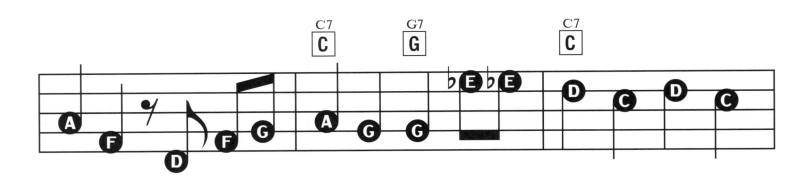

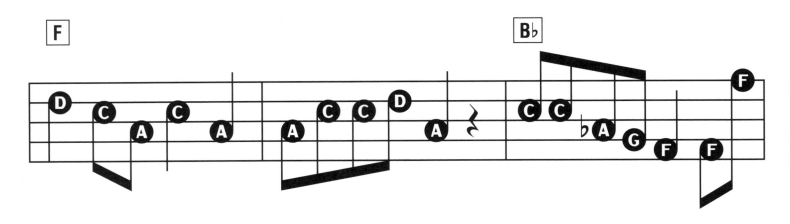

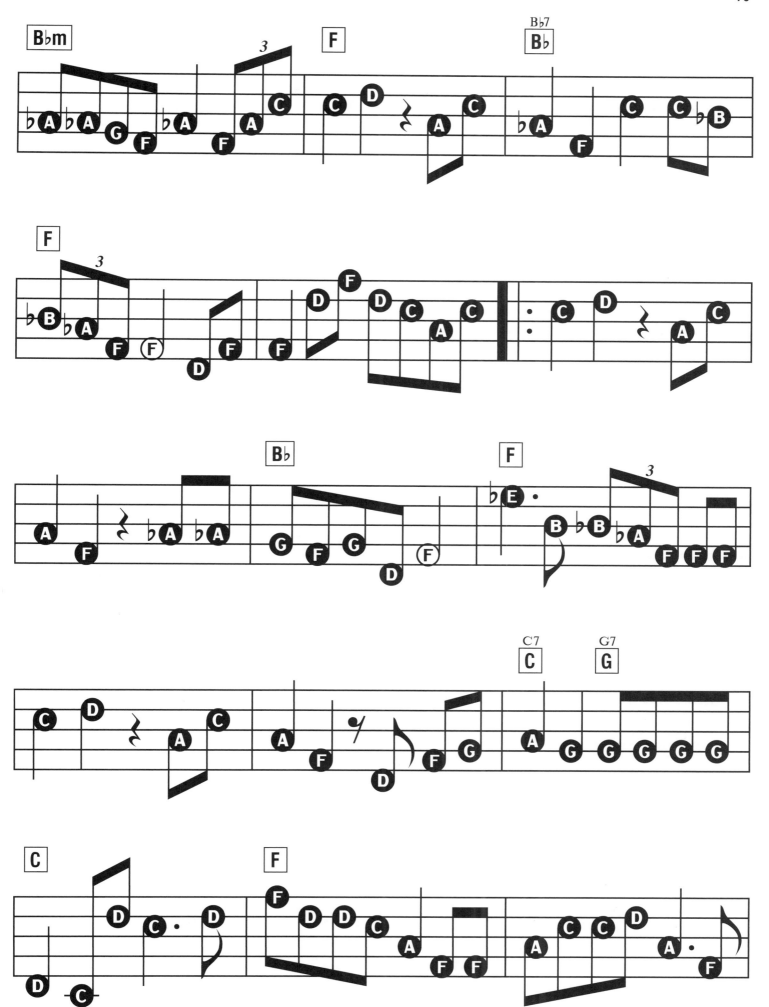

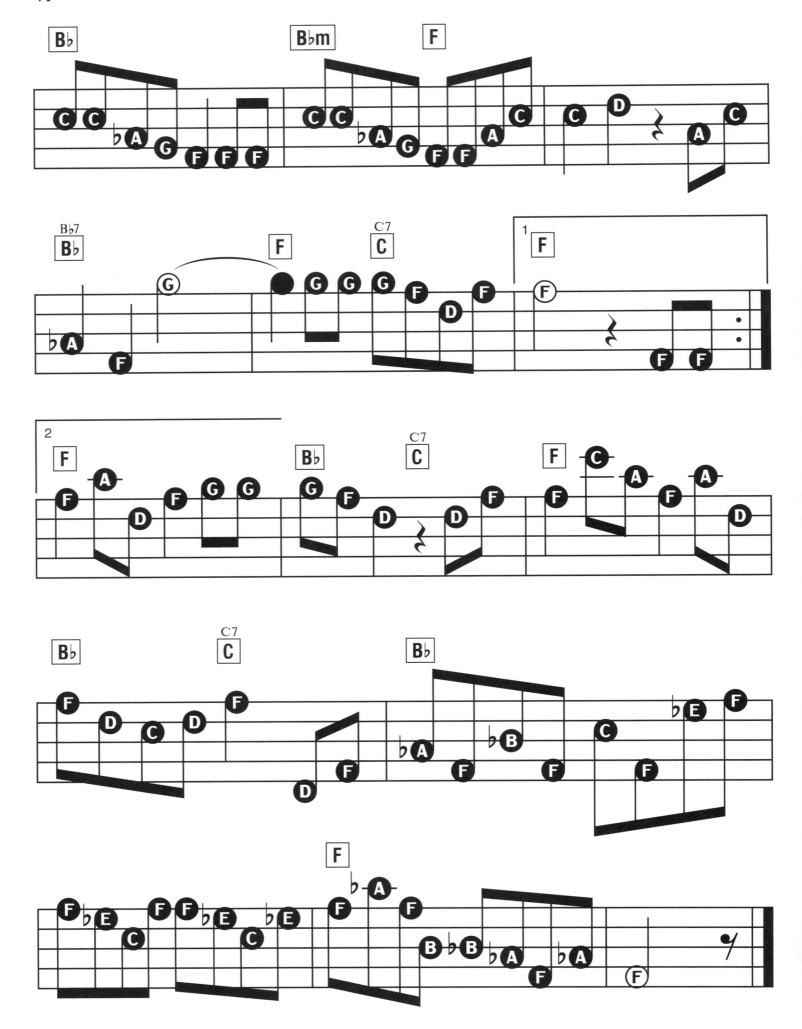

Playboy's Theme

Registration 8
Rhythm: Swing

Music by Cy Coleman

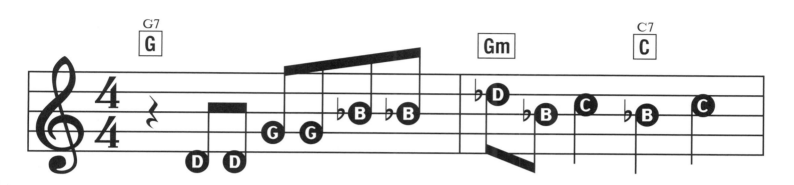

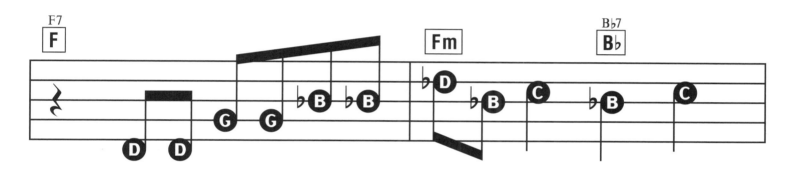

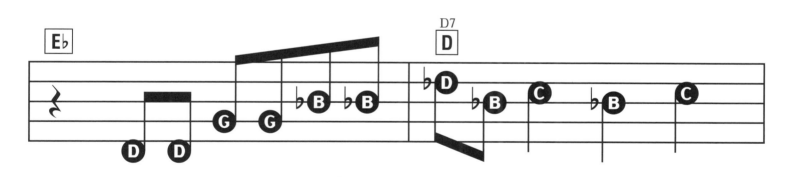

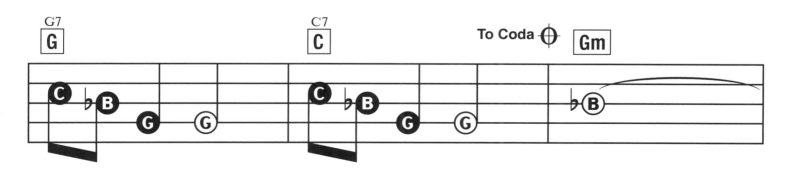

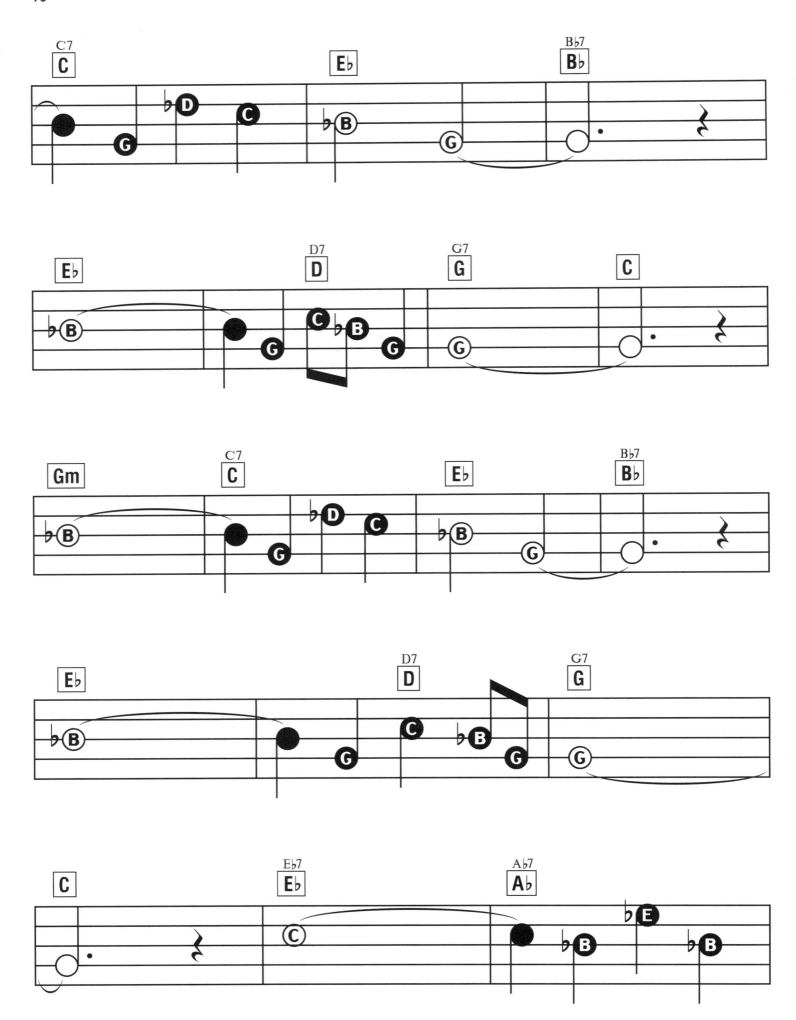

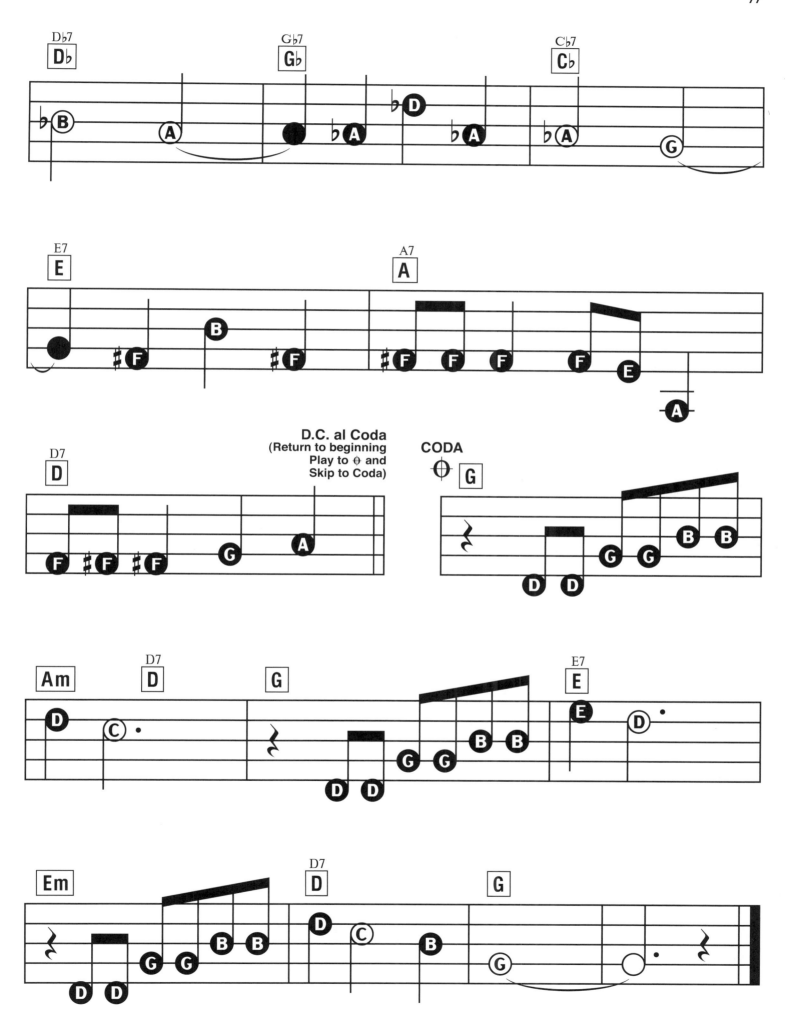

Pick Up the Pieces

Words and Music by James Hamish Stuart,
Alan Gorrie, Roger Ball, Robbie McIntosh,
Owen McIntyre and Malcolm Duncan

Registration 4
Rhythm: Funk or Rock

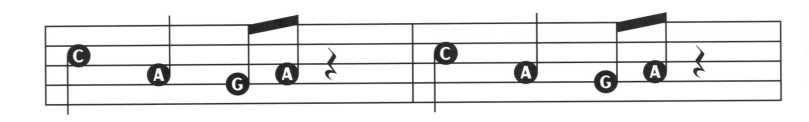

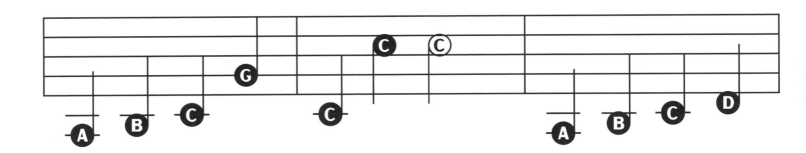

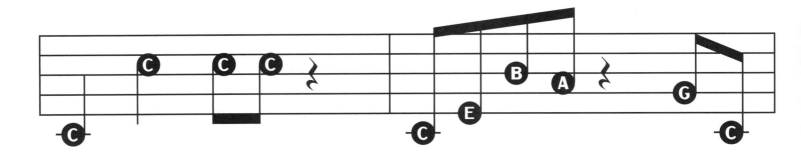

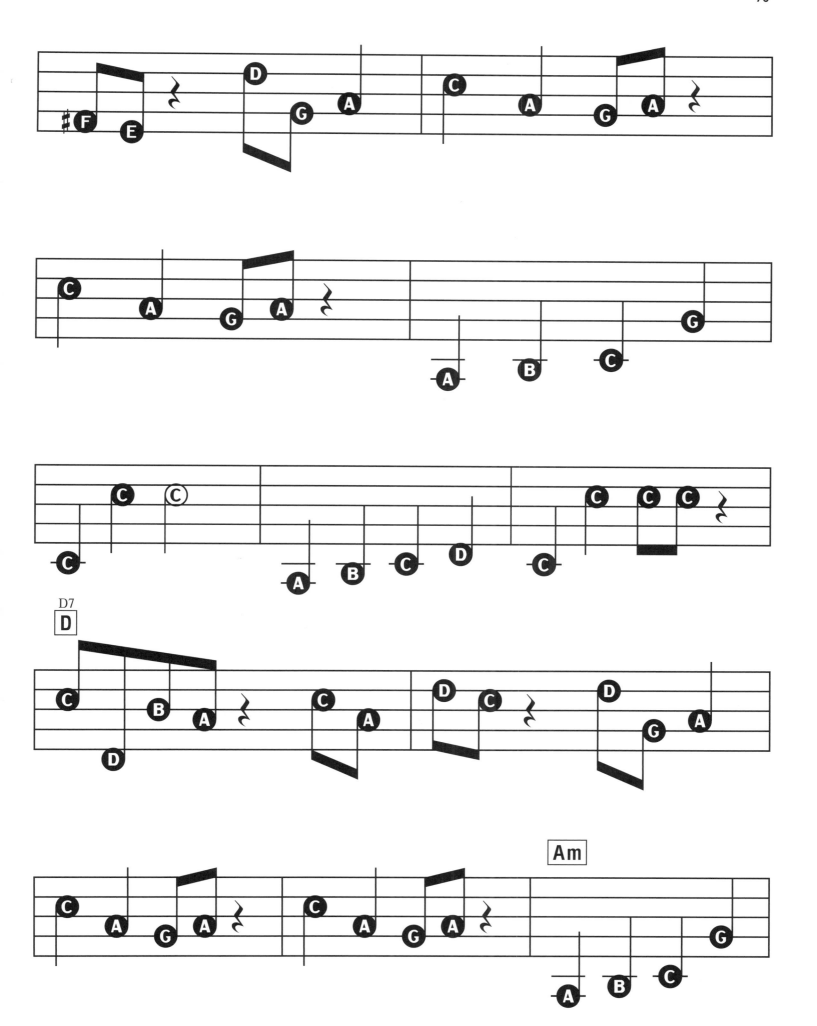

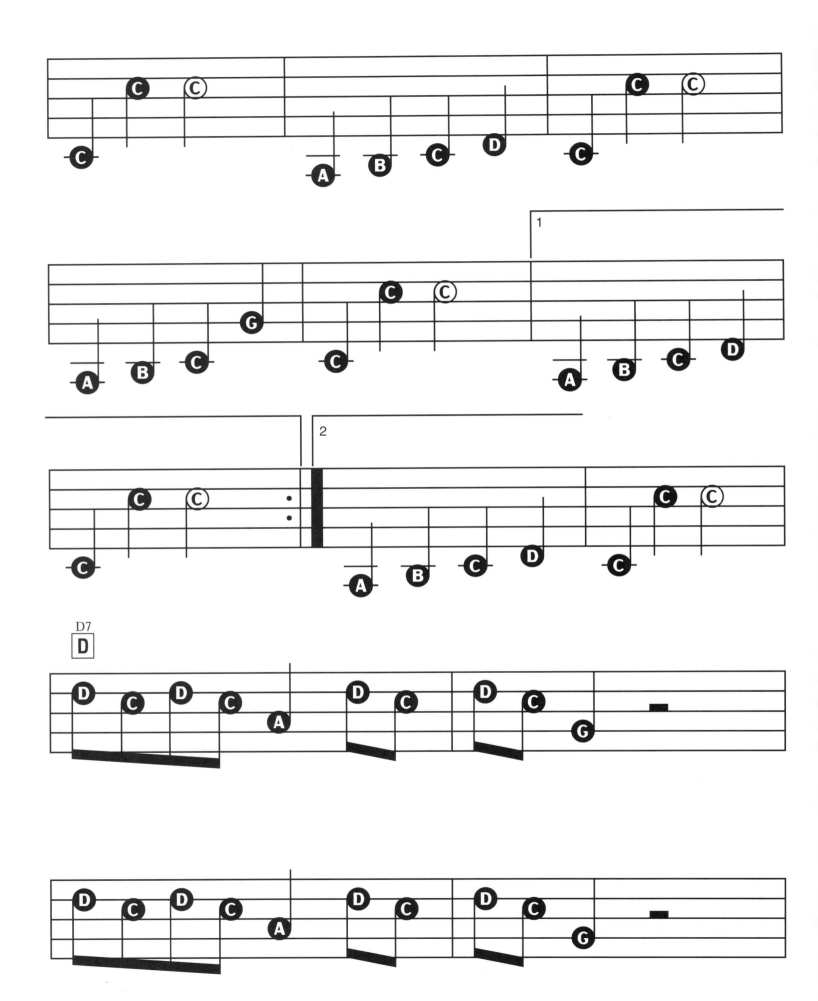

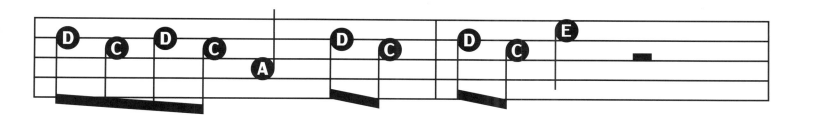

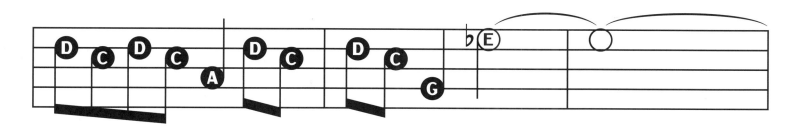

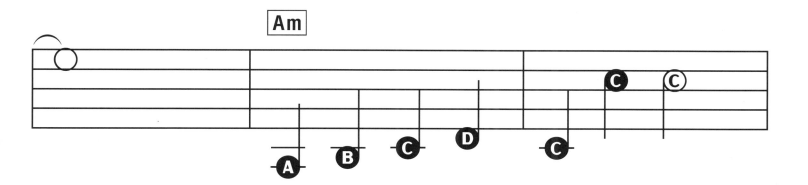

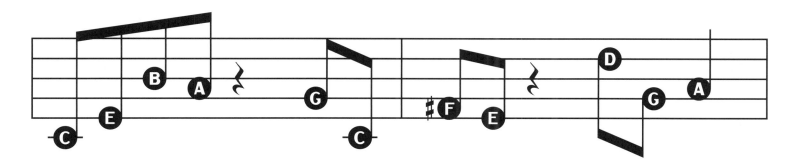

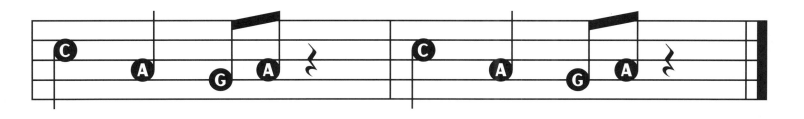

Reunion Blues

Registration 5
Rhythm: Swing

By Milt Jackson

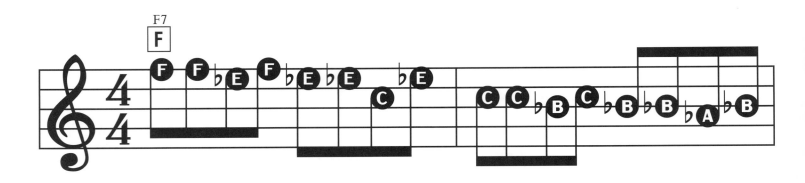

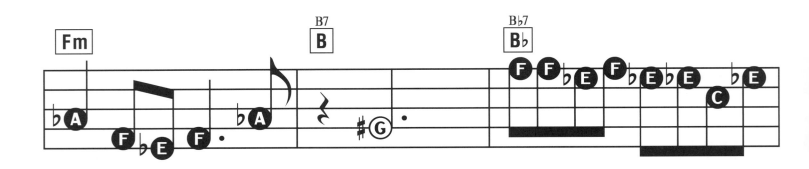

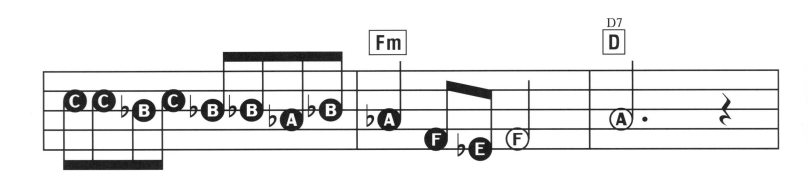

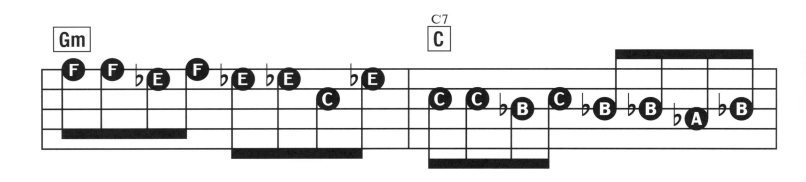

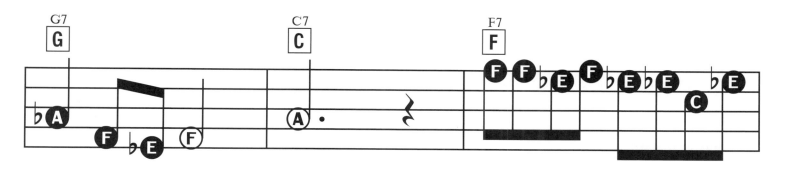

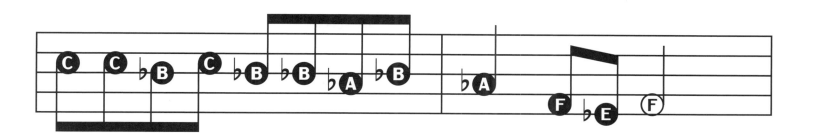

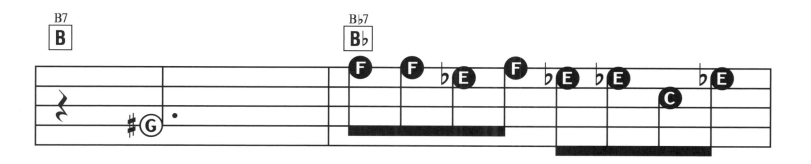

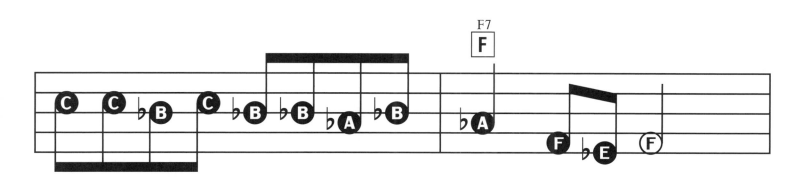

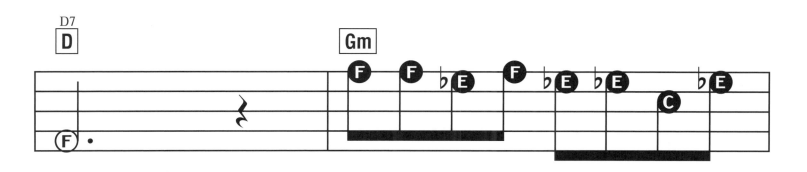

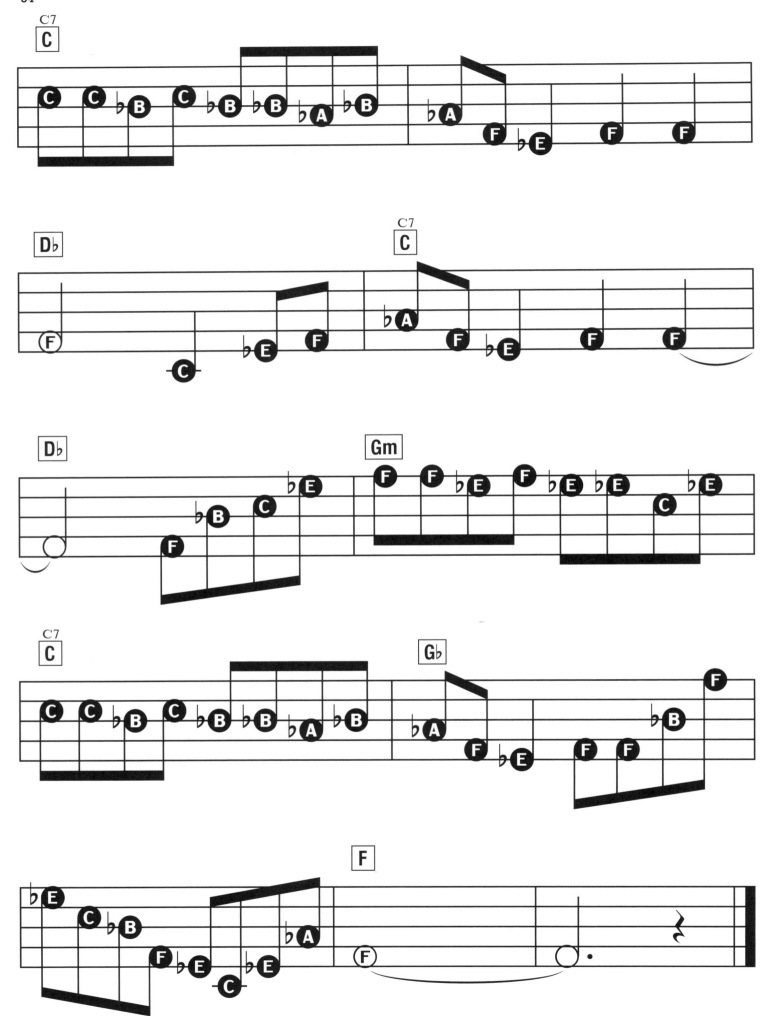

Rockin' in Rhythm

Registration 3
Rhythm: Swing

By Duke Ellington, Irving Mills
and Harry Carney

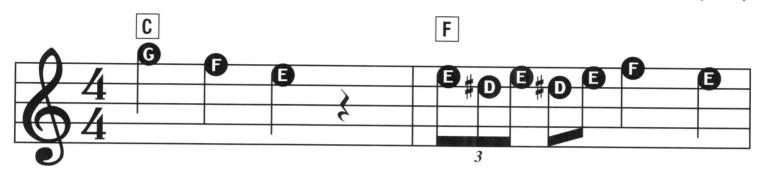

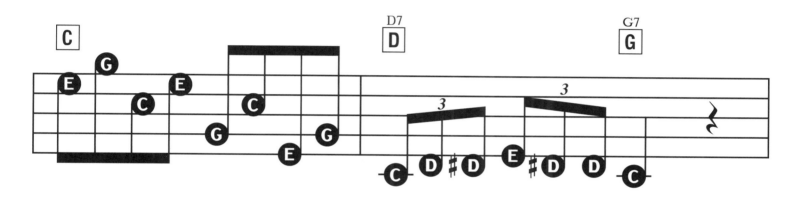

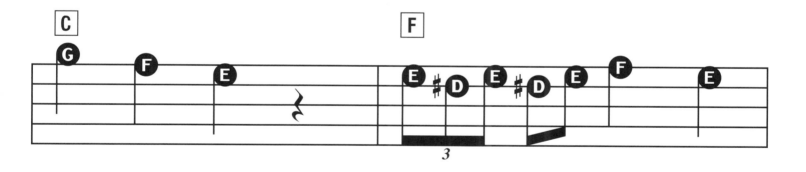

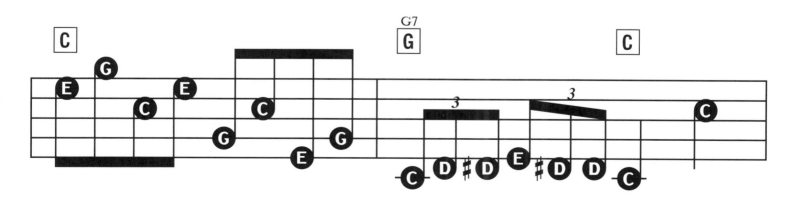

86

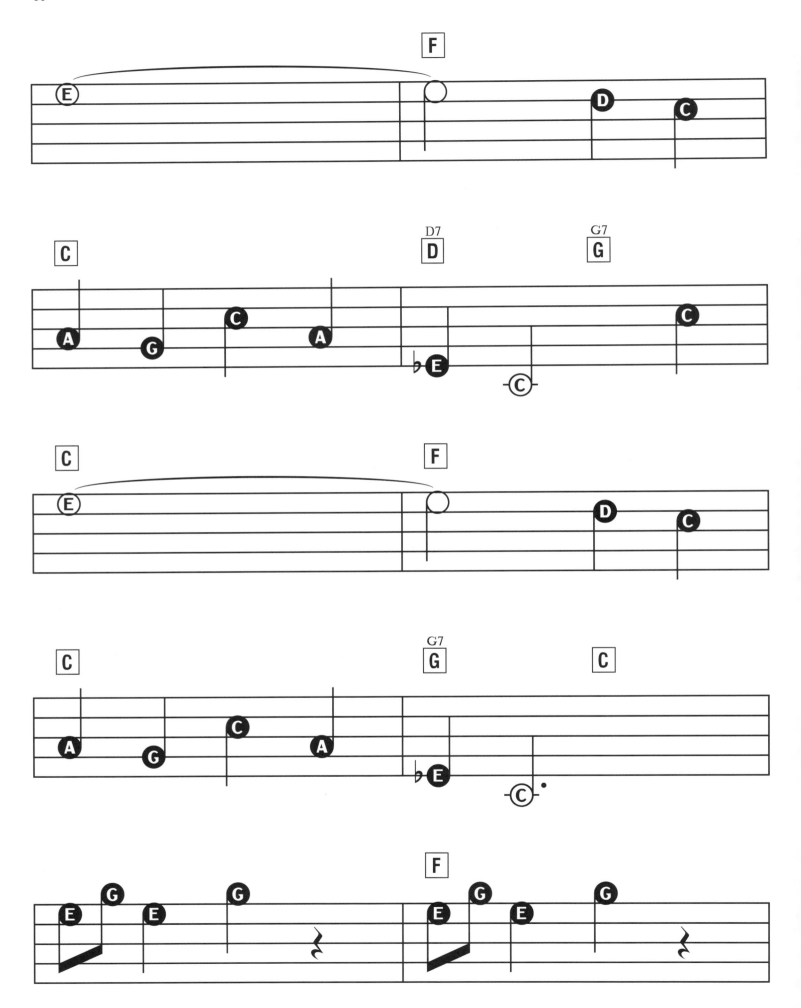

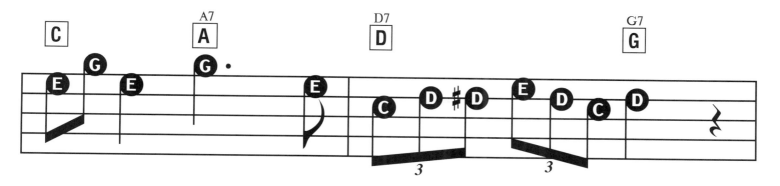

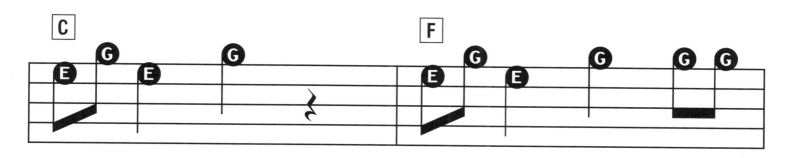

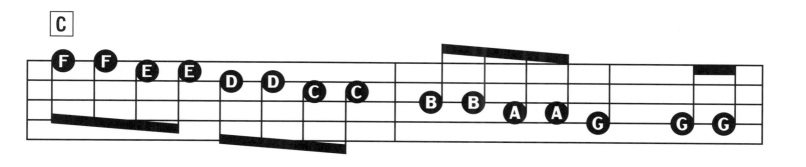

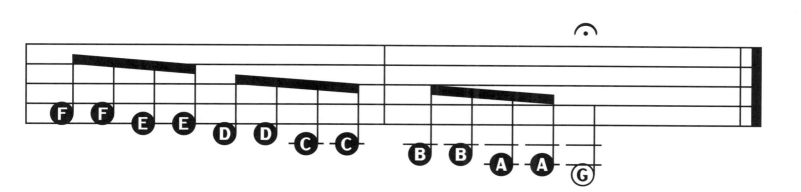

Robbin's Nest

Registration 7
Rhythm: Swing

By Sir Charles Thompson
and Illinois Jacquet

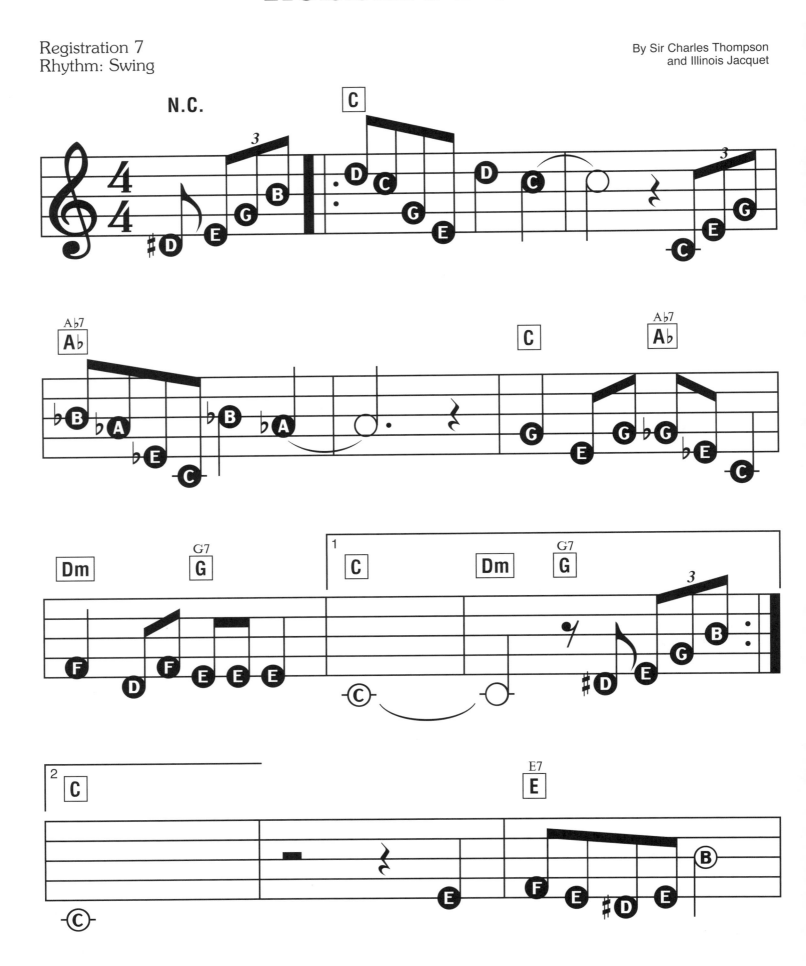

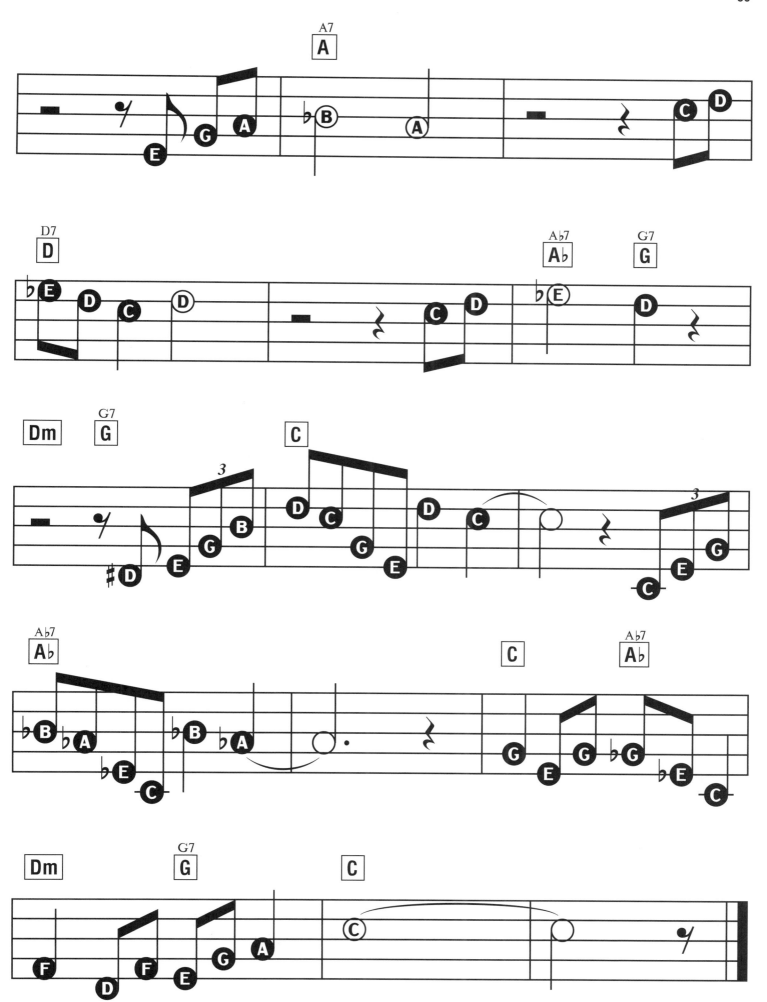

Ruby, My Dear

Registration 1
Rhythm: Ballad

By Thelonious Monk

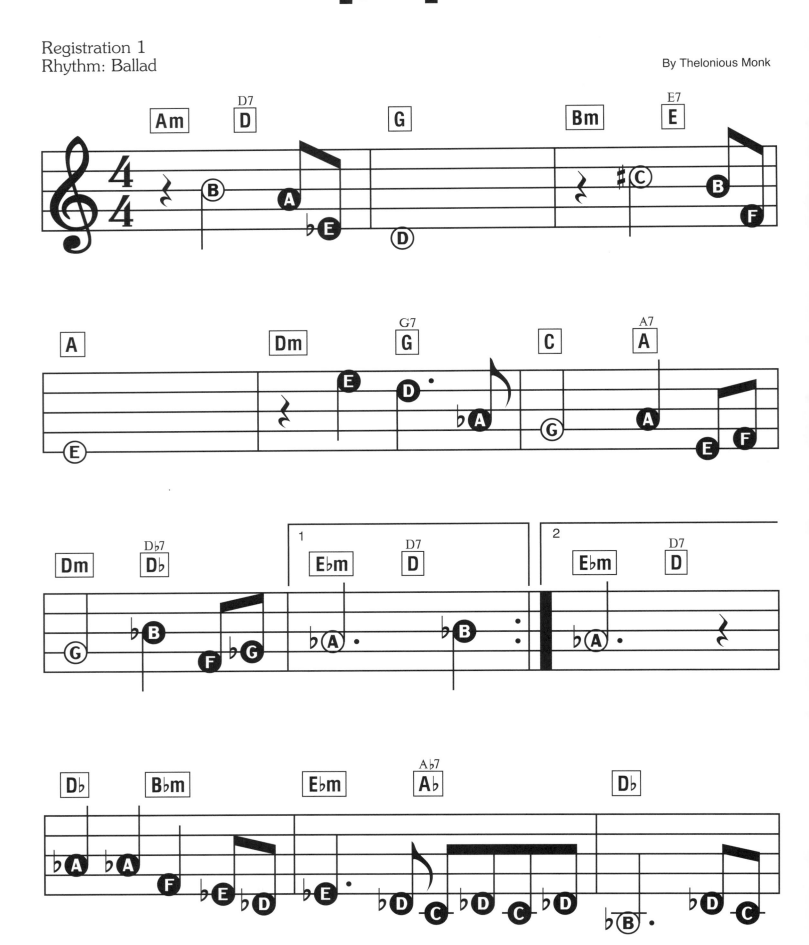

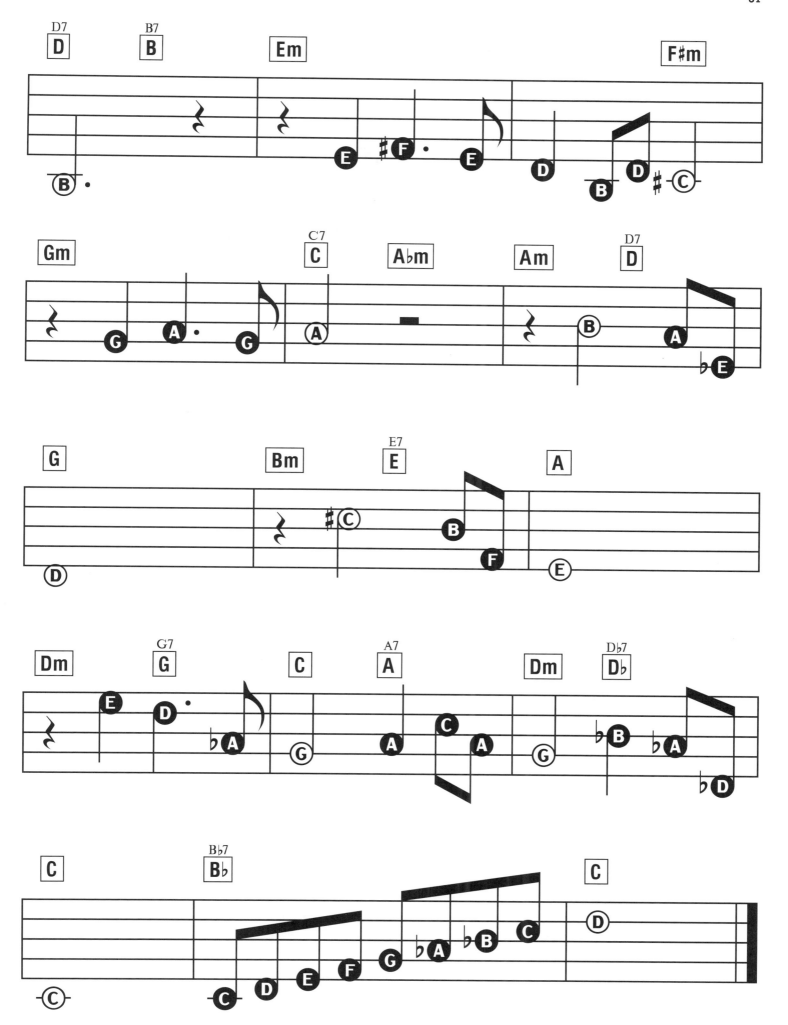

St. Thomas

Registration 5
Rhythm: Calypso or Latin

By Sonny Rollins

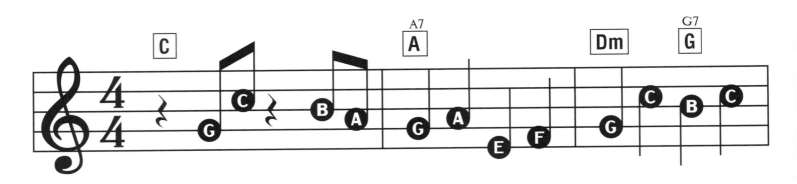

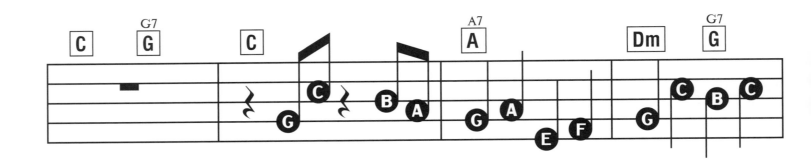

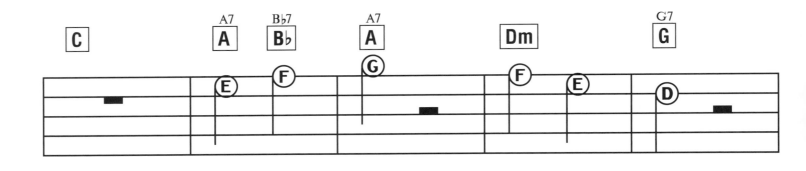

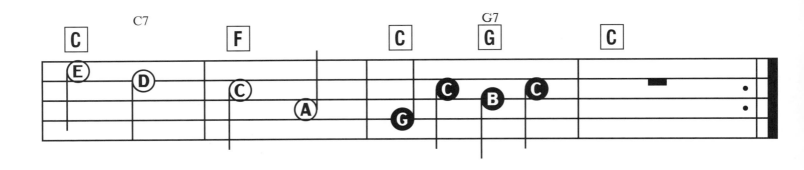

Save the Bones for Henry Jones

Registration 7
Rhythm: Swing

Words and Music by Danny Barker
and Vernon Lee

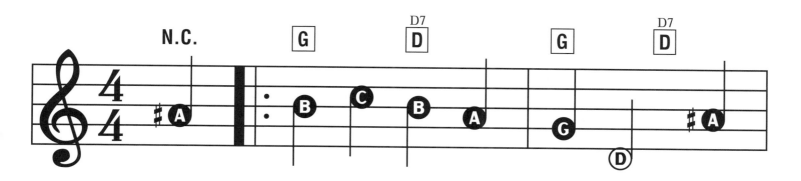

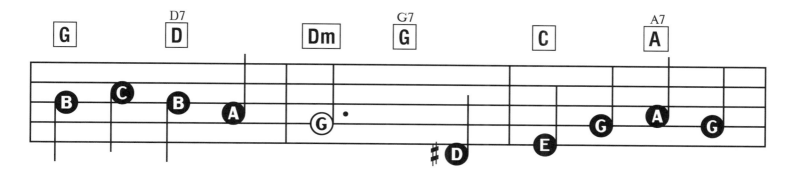

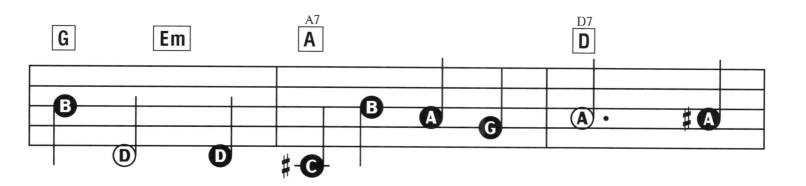

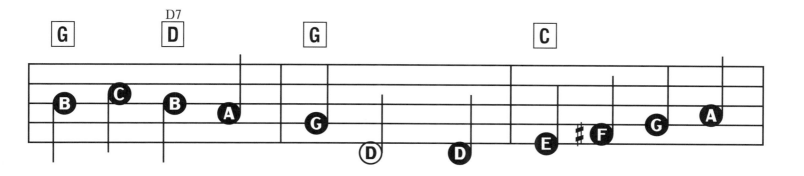

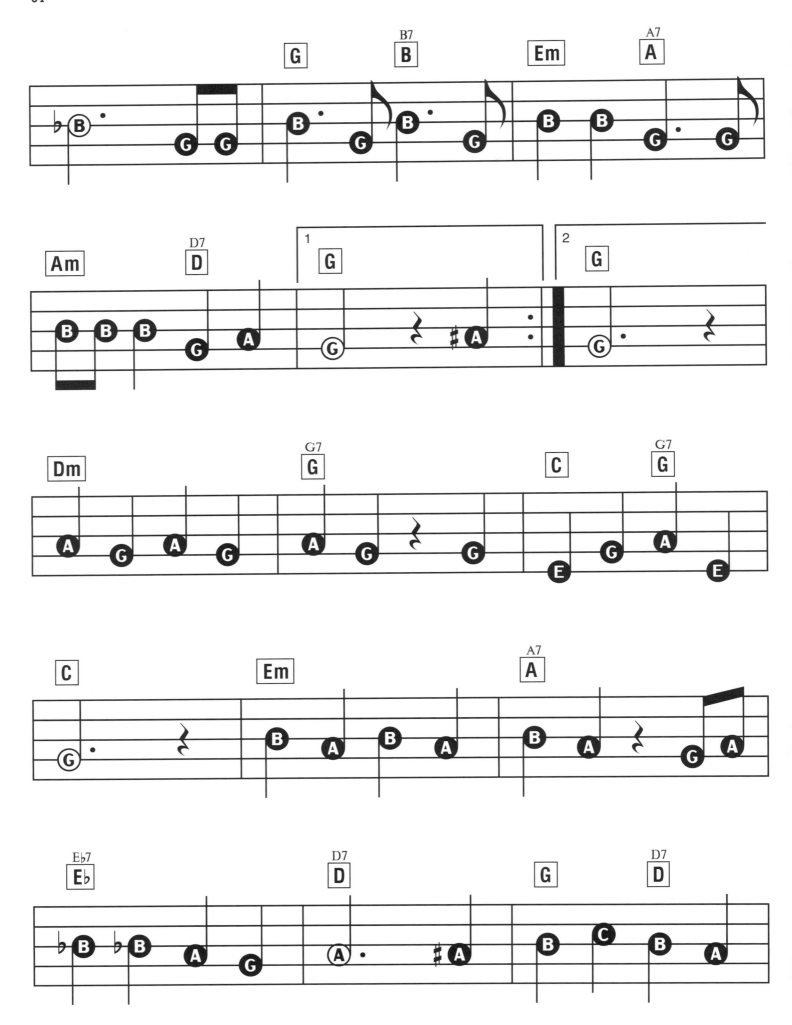

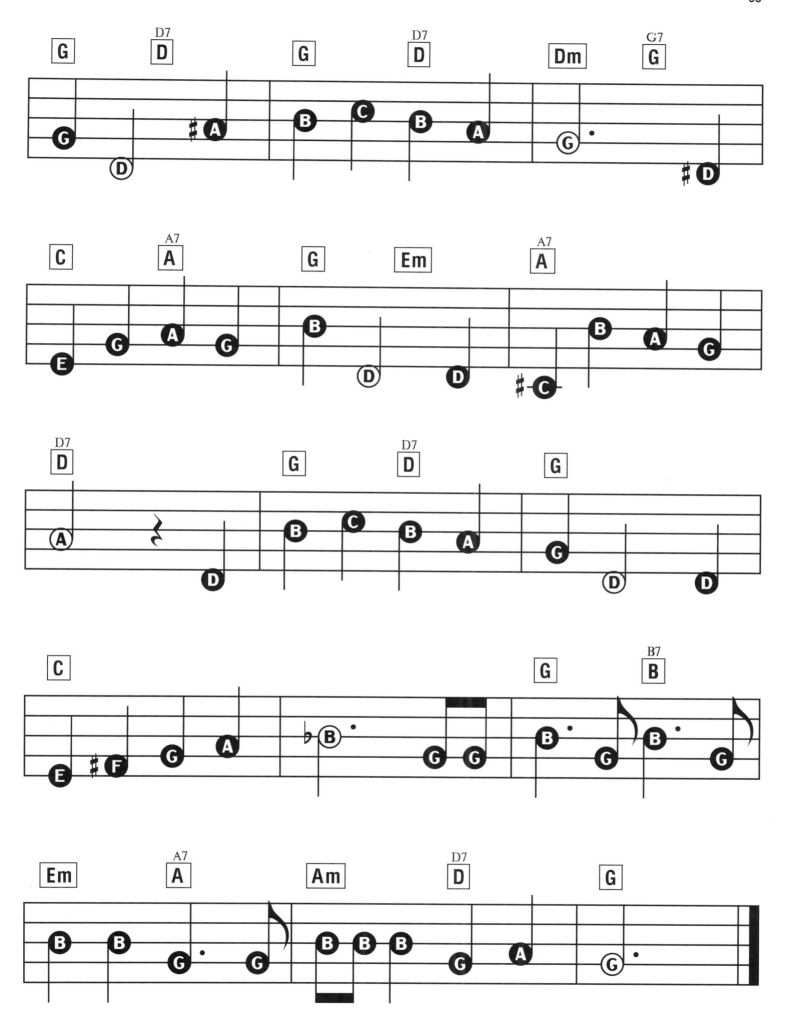

Shiny Stockings

Registration 8
Rhythm: Swing

Music by Frank Foster

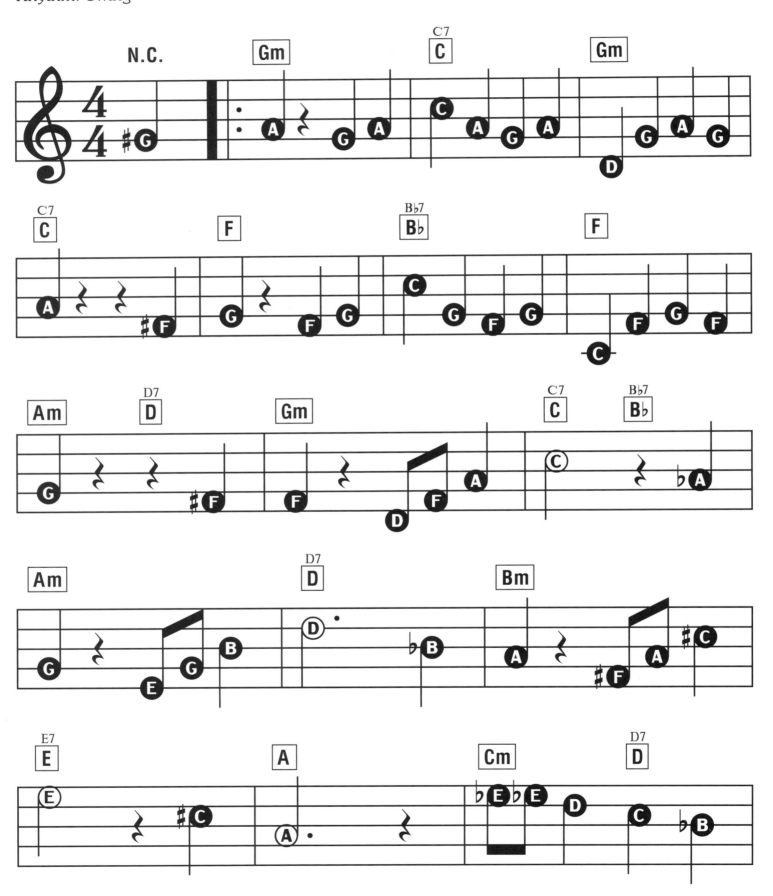

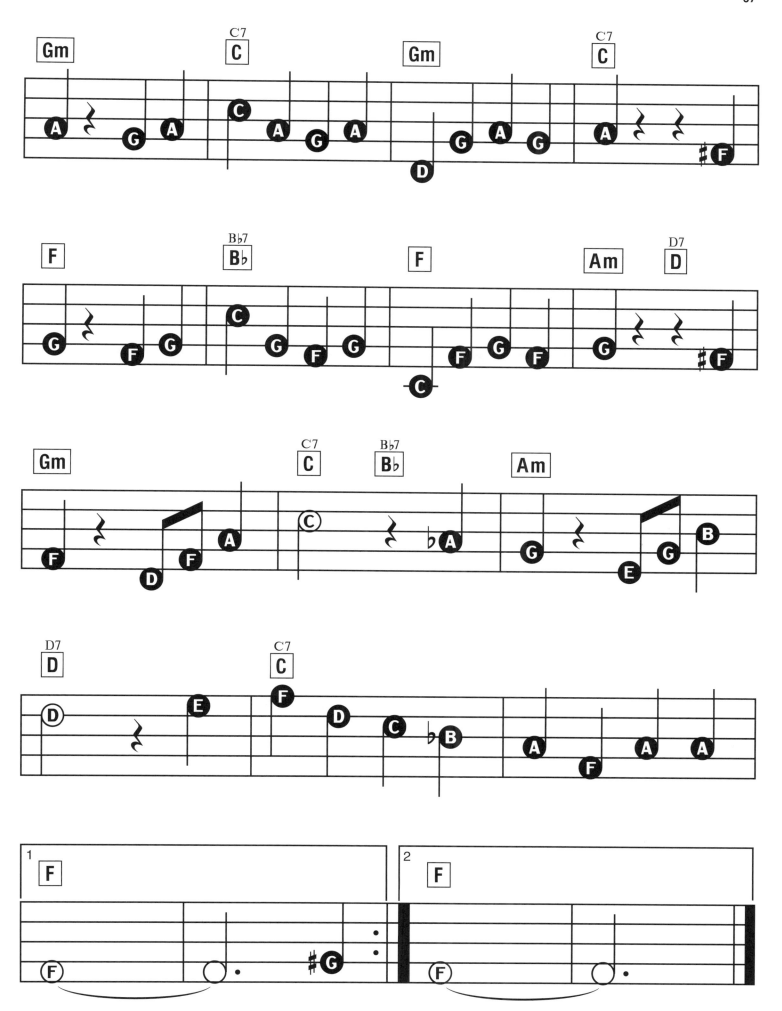

Sidewinder

Registration 7
Rhythm: Rock

By Lee Morgan

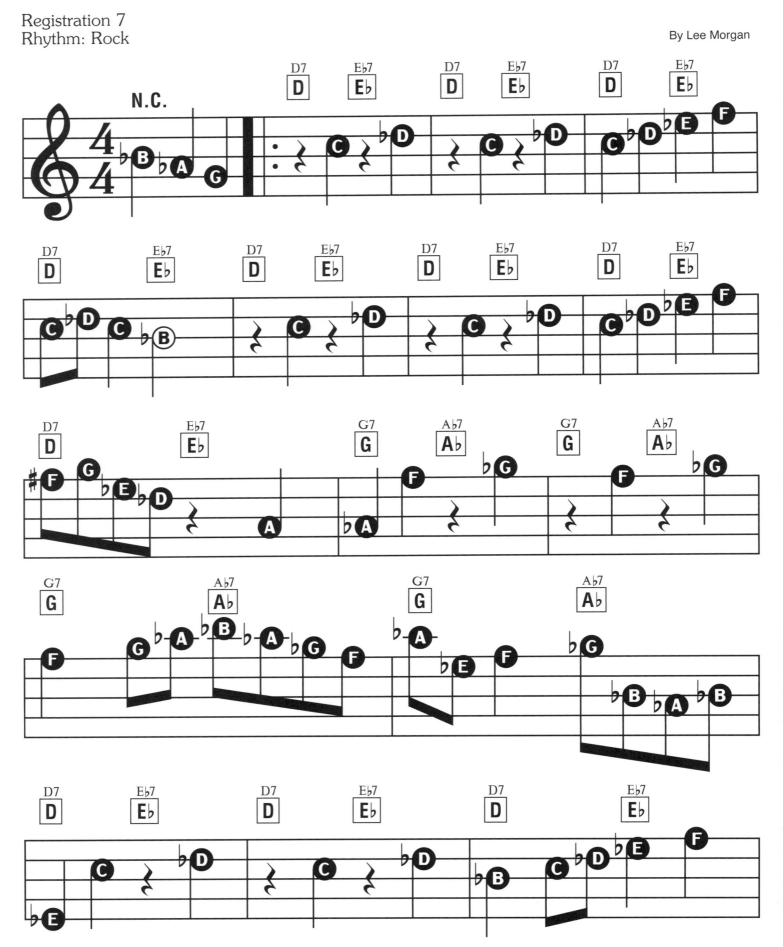

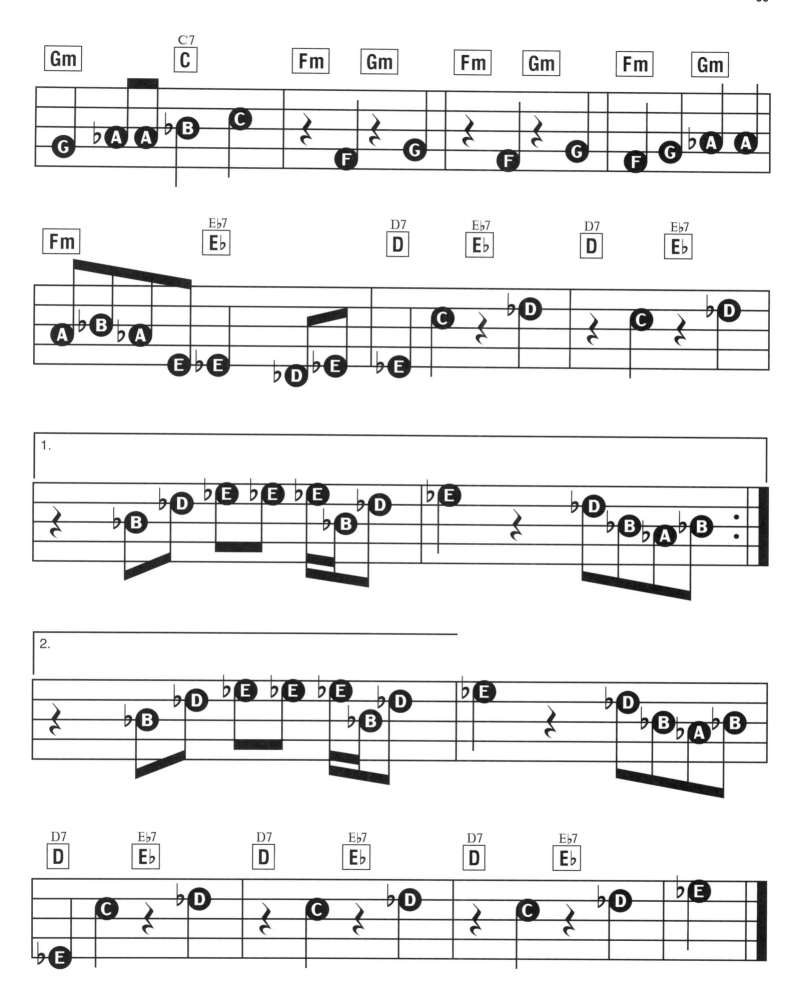

Skating in Central Park

Registration 7
Rhythm: Jazz Waltz or Waltz

By John Lewis

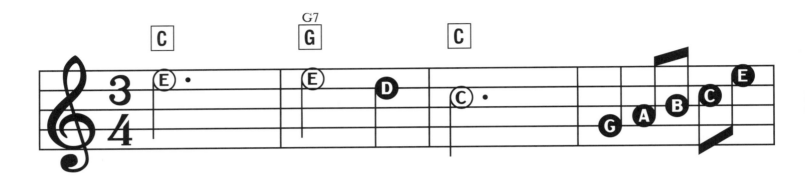

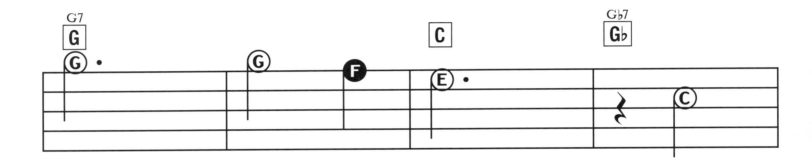

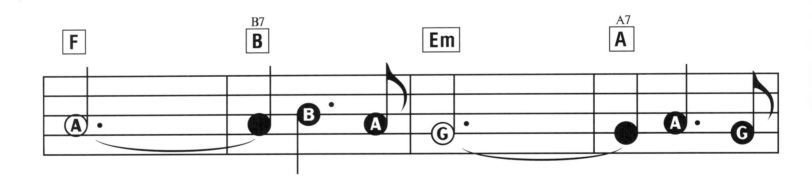

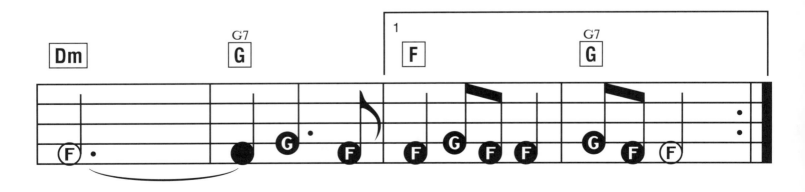

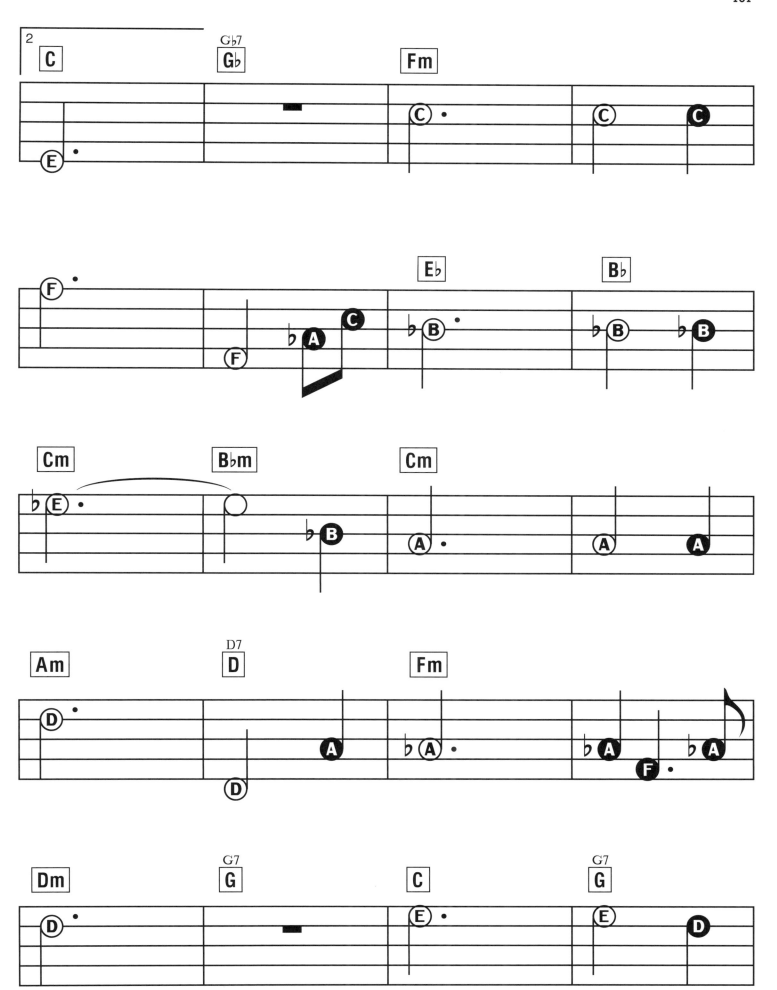

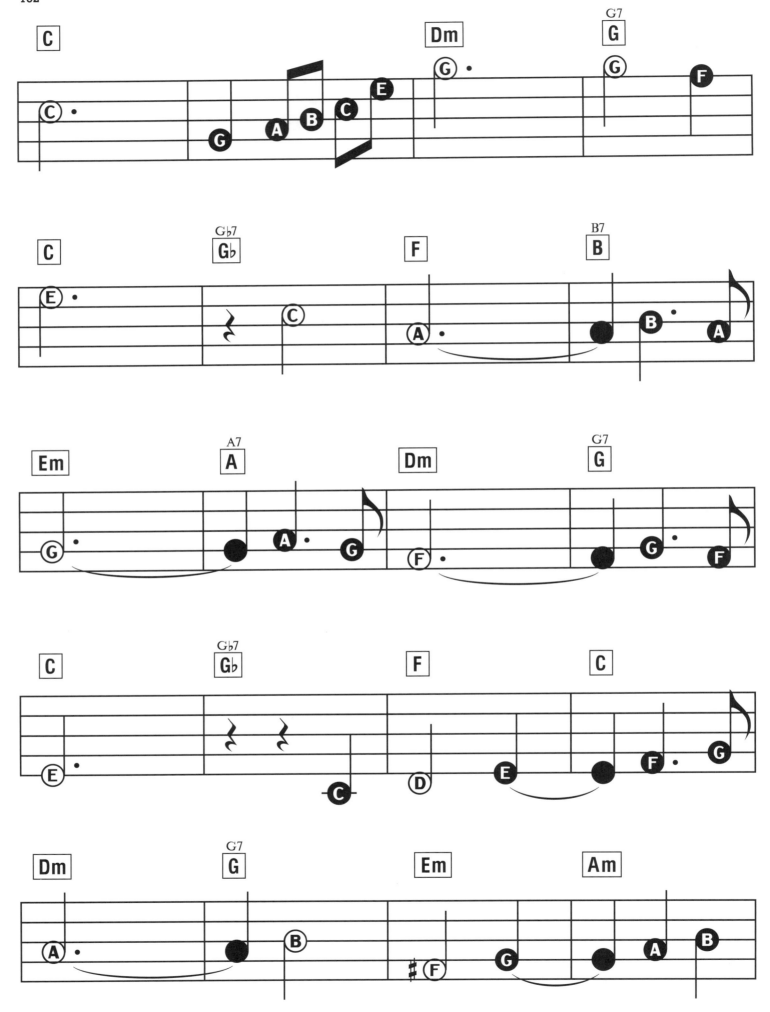

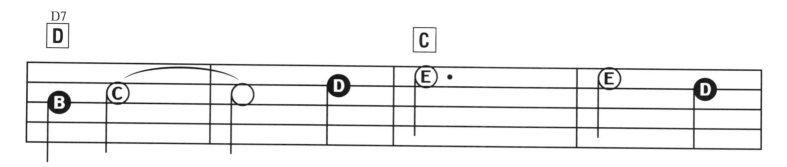

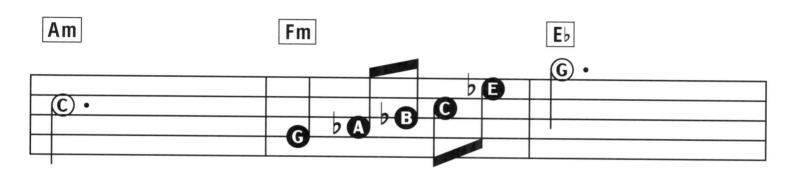

No Rhythm

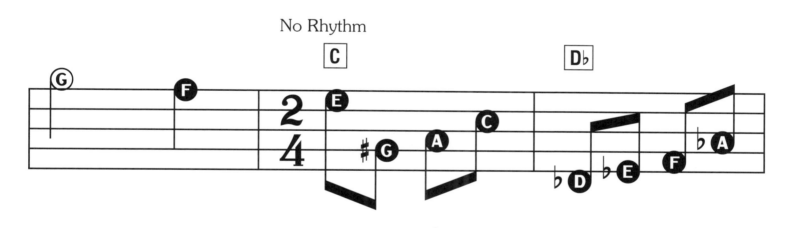

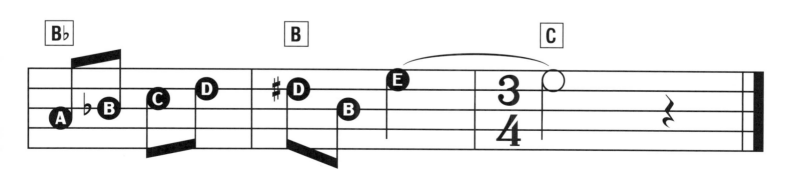

Song for My Father

Registration 8
Rhythm: Latin

Words and Music by
Horace Silver

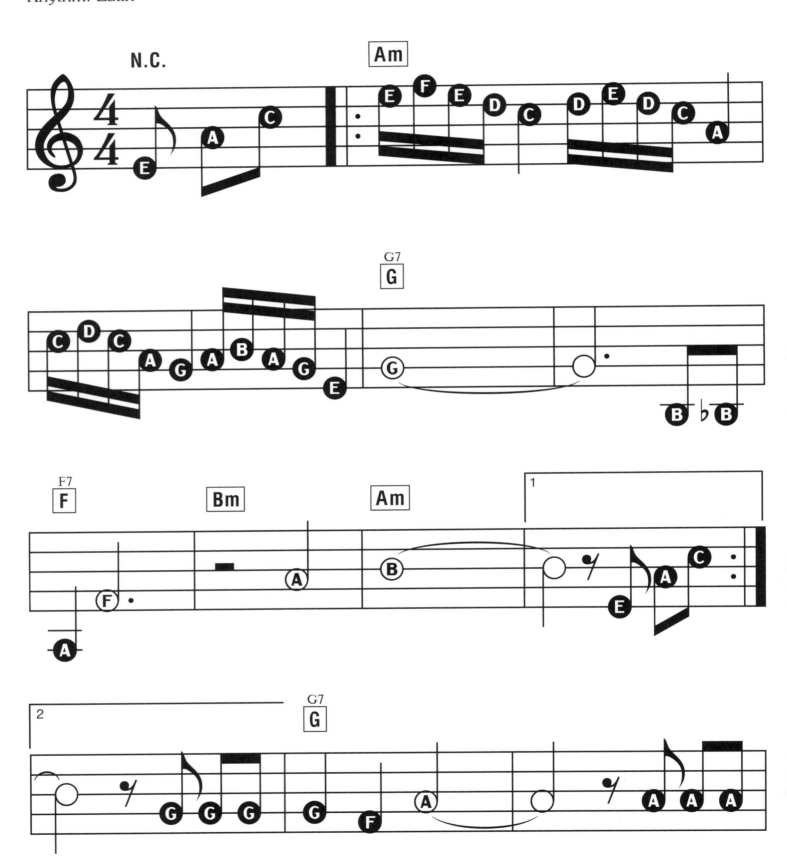

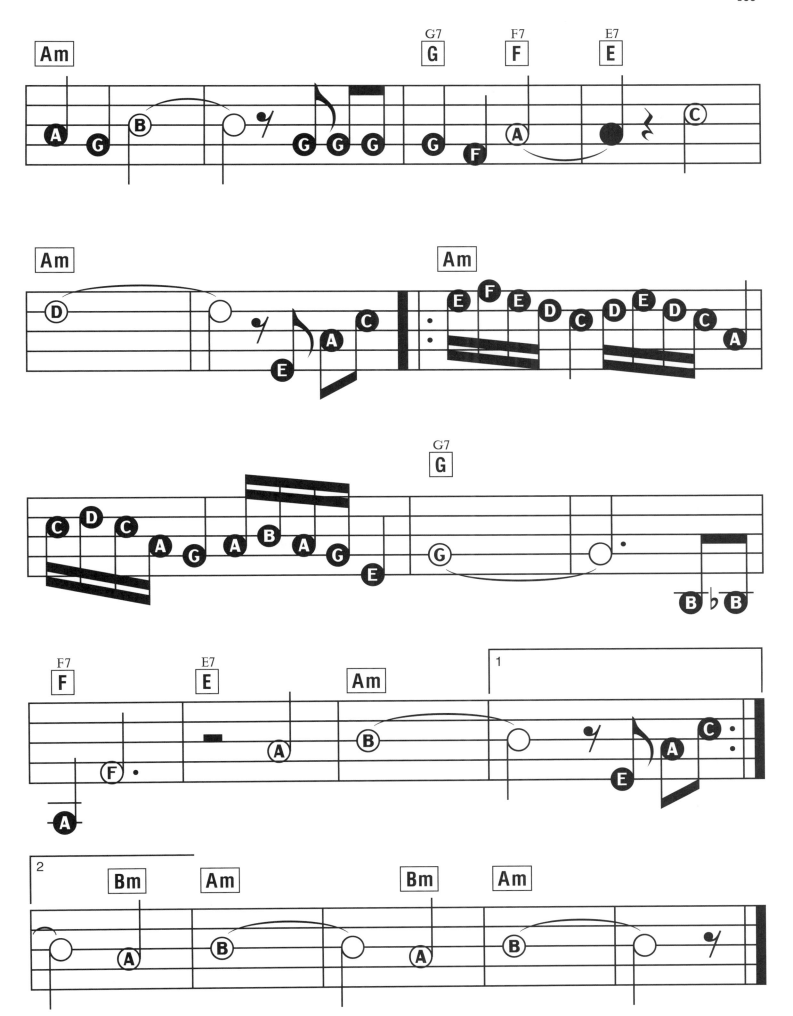

Stolen Moments

Registration 4
Rhythm: Swing

Words and Music by
Oliver Nelson

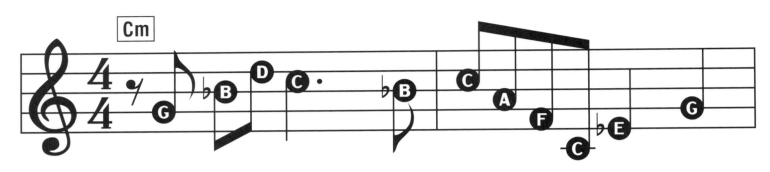

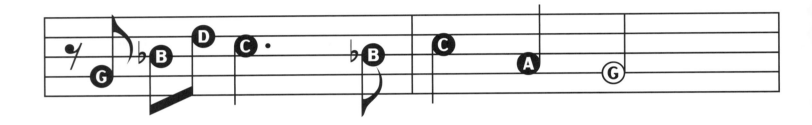

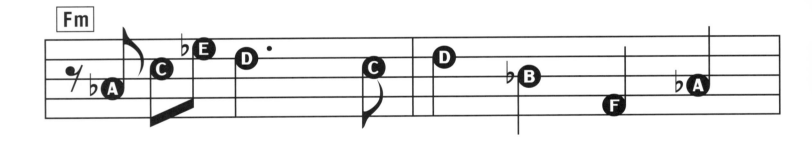

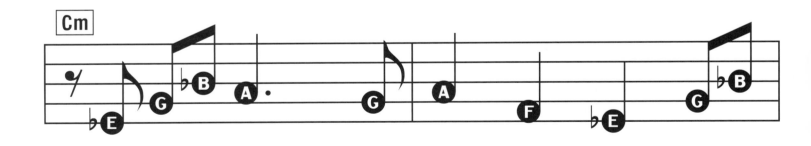

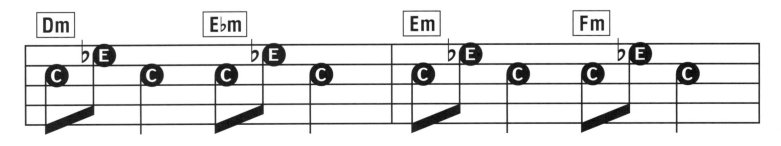

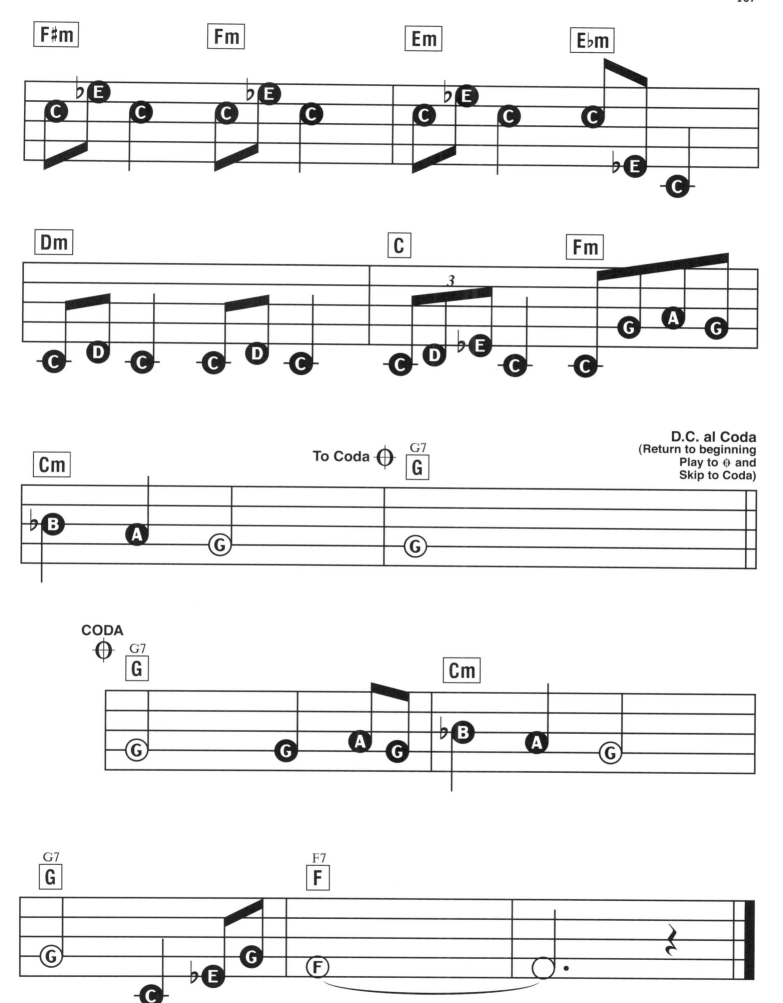

Street Life

Registration 8
Rhythm: Funk or Rock

Words and Music by Will Jennings
and Joe Sample

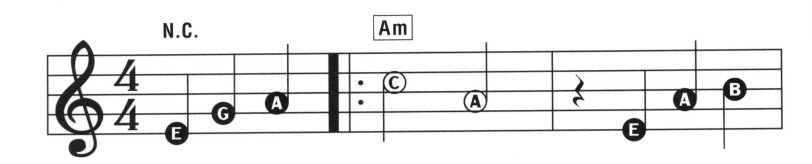

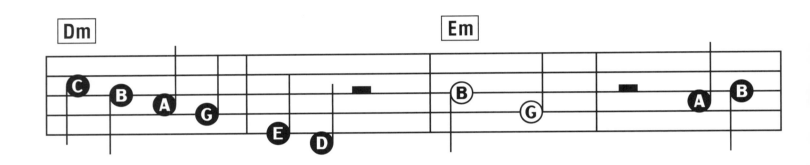

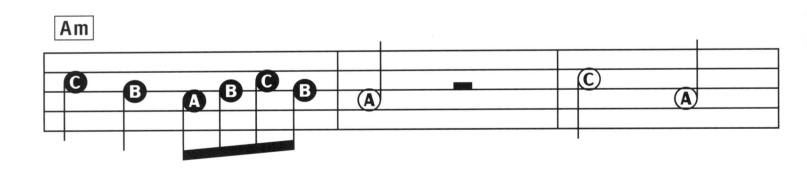

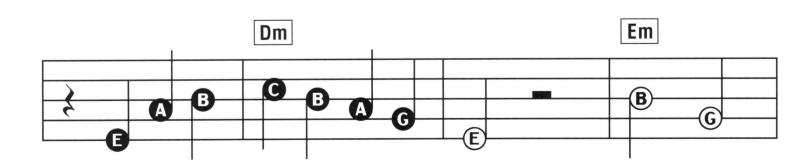

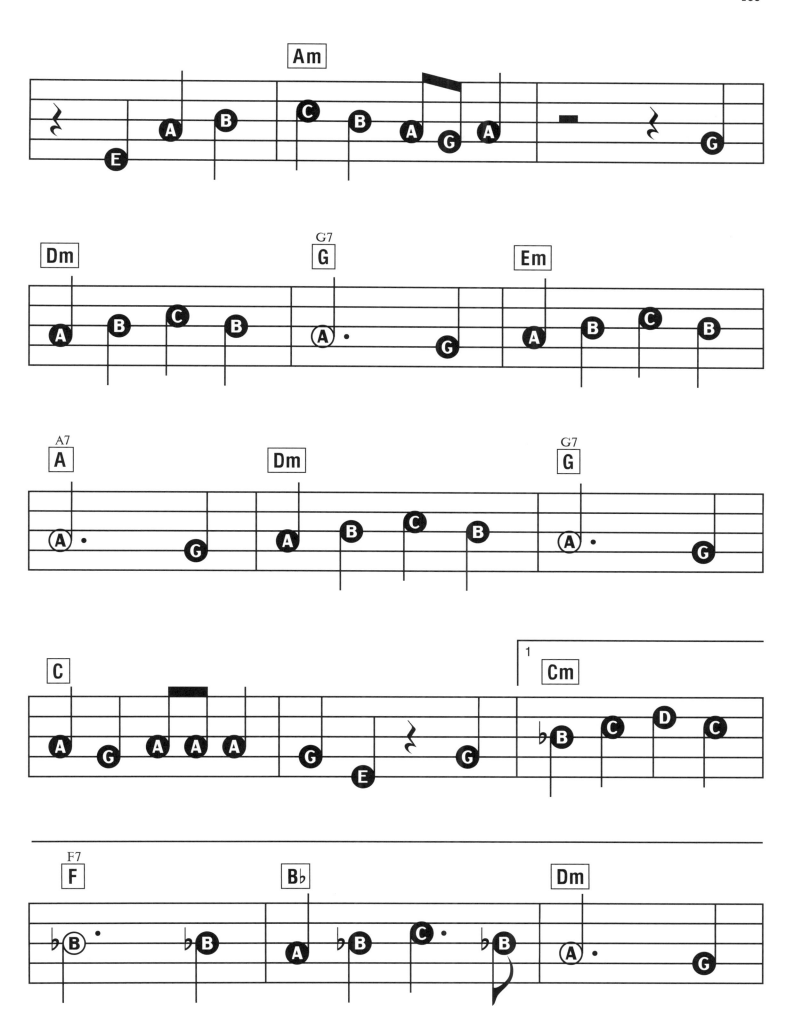

110

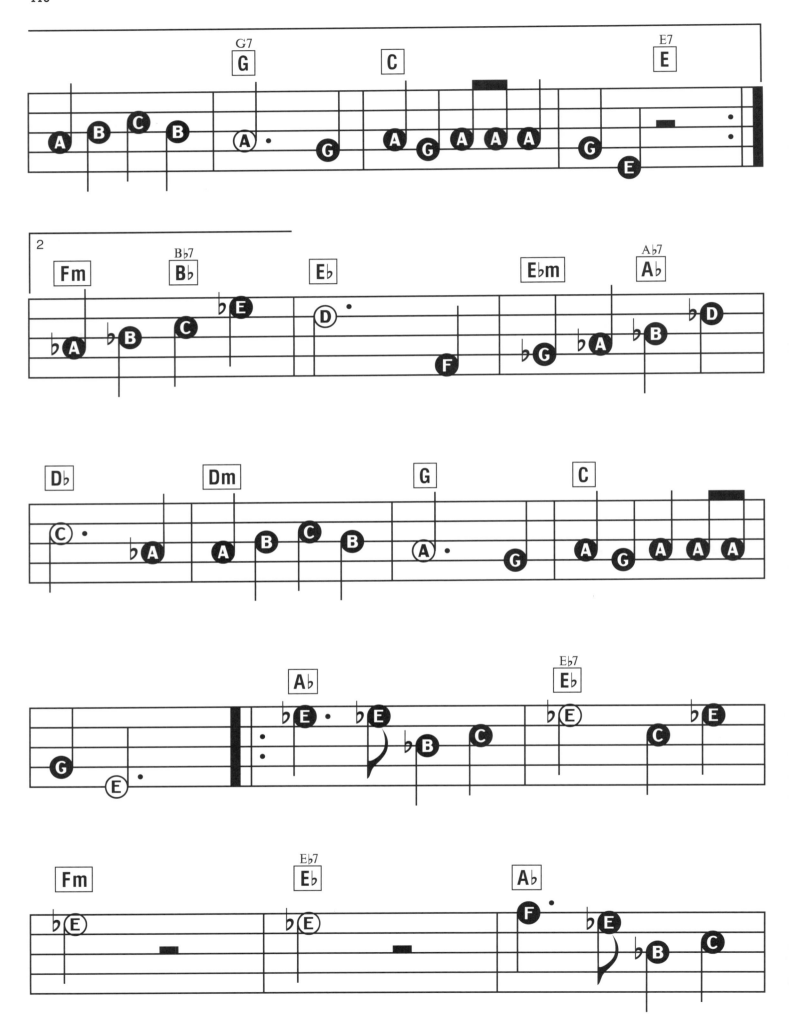

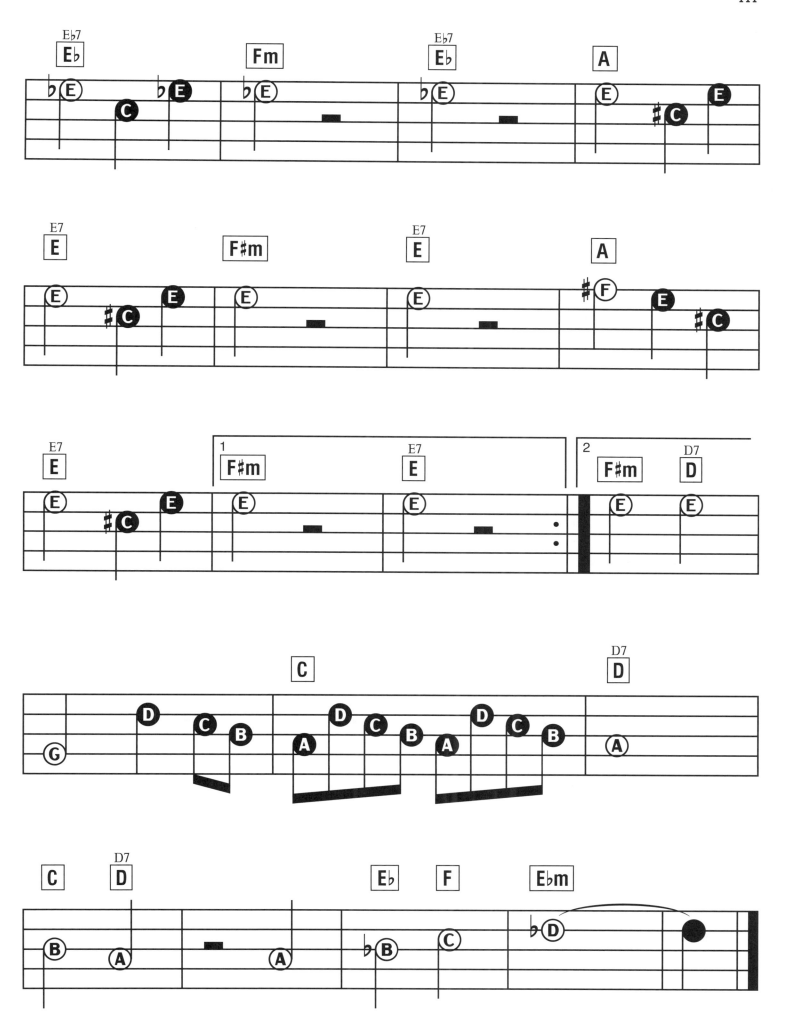

Things Ain't What They Used to Be

Registration 1
Rhythm: Swing

By Mercer Ellington

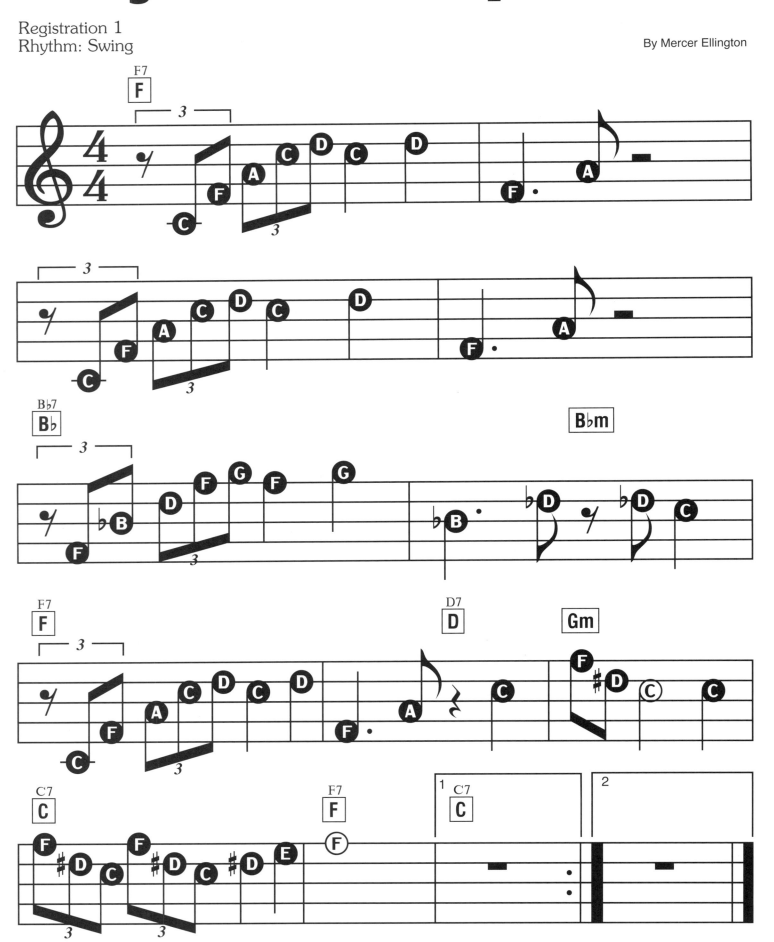

Waltz for Debby

Registration 8
Rhythm: Jazz Waltz or Waltz

Lyric by Gene Lees
Music by Bill Evans

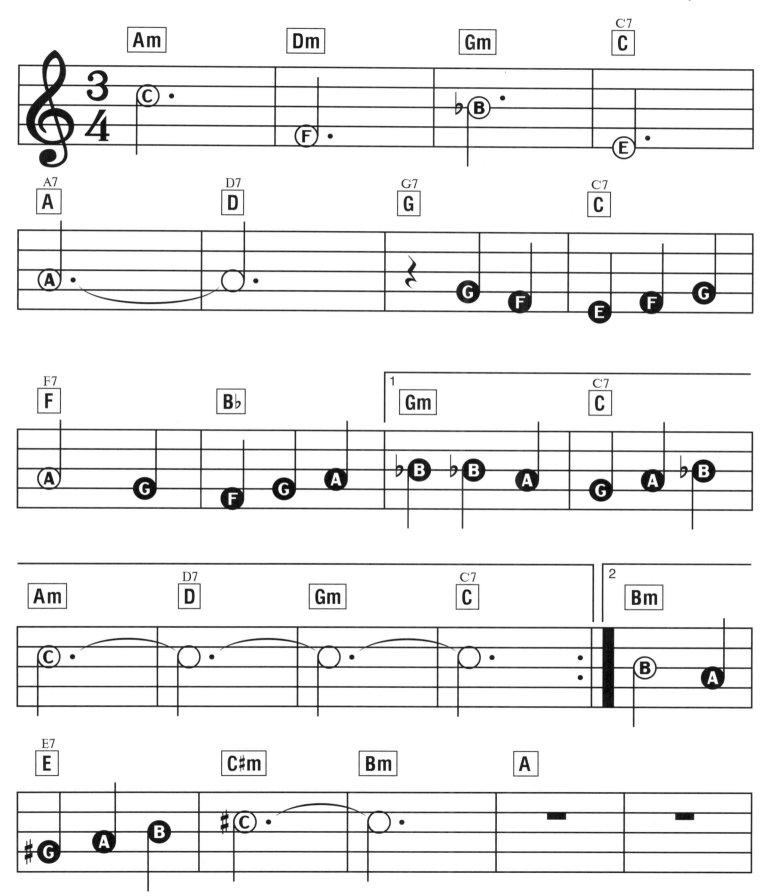

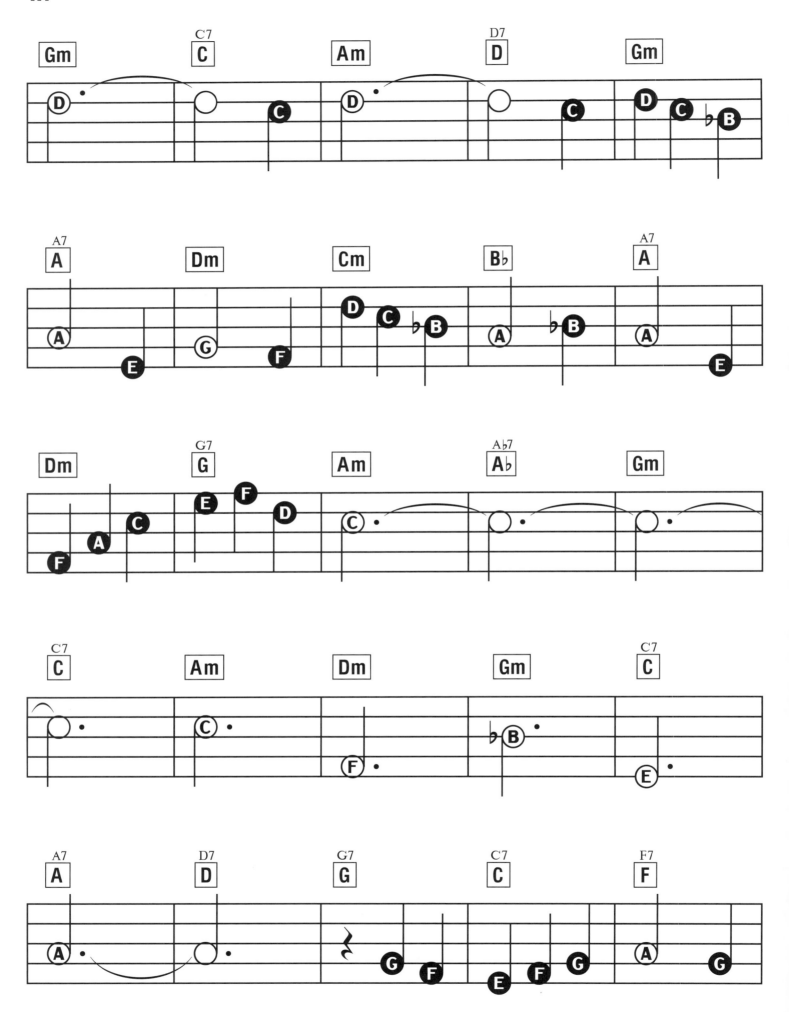

115

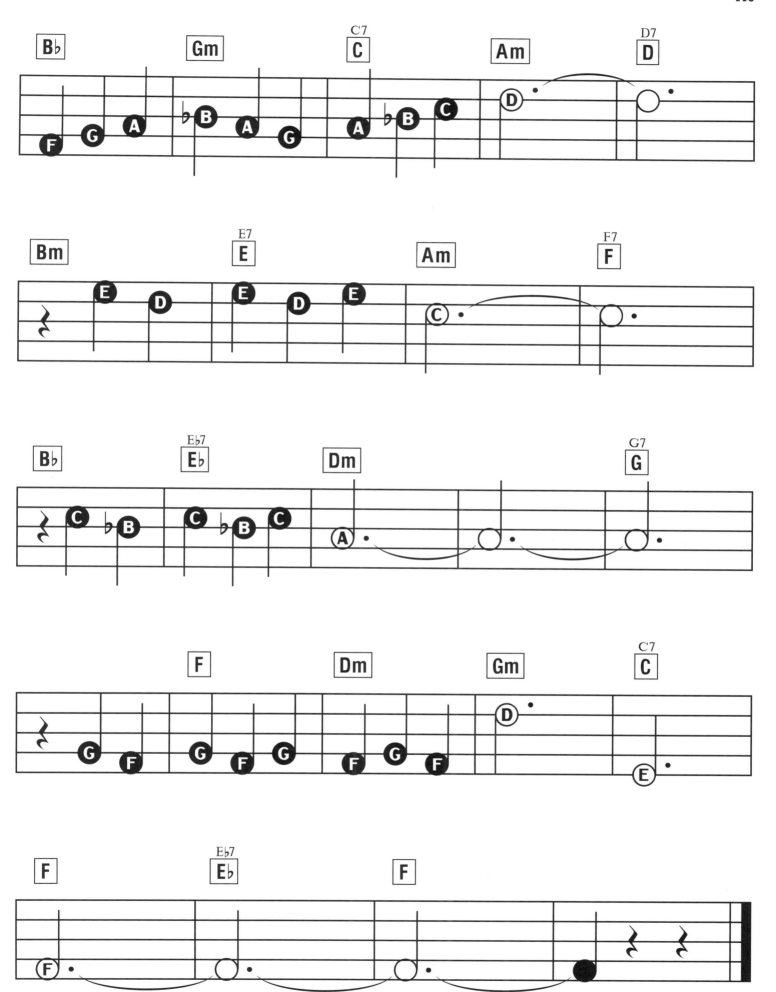

Topsy

Registration 7
Rhythm: Swing

Written by Edgar Battle
and Eddie Durham

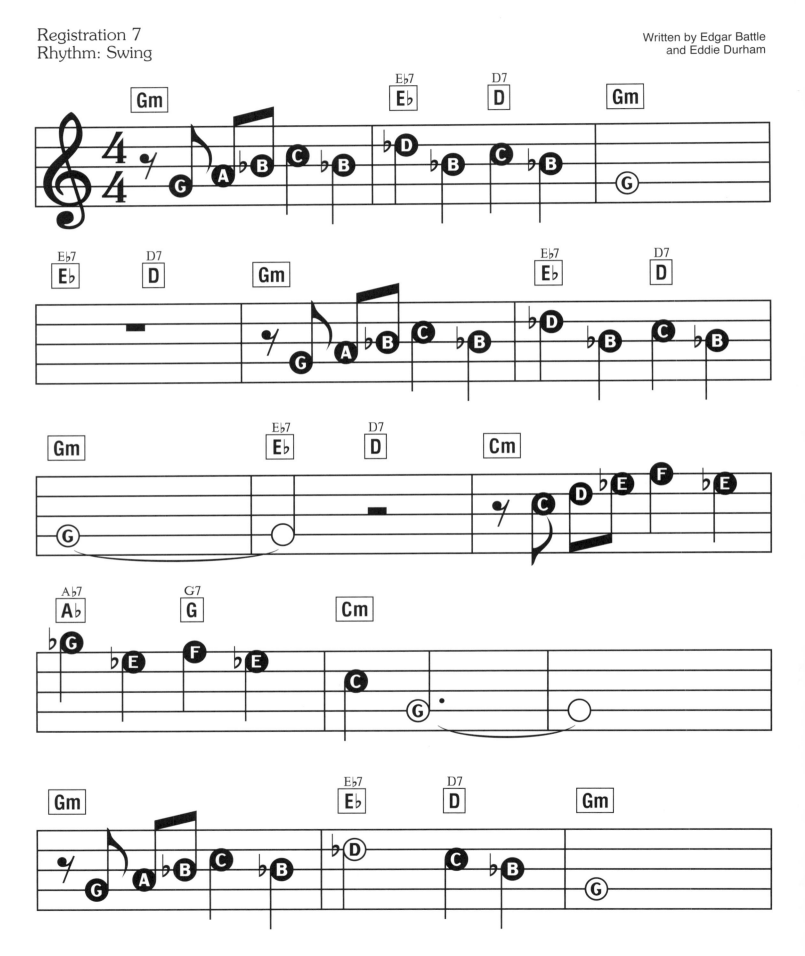

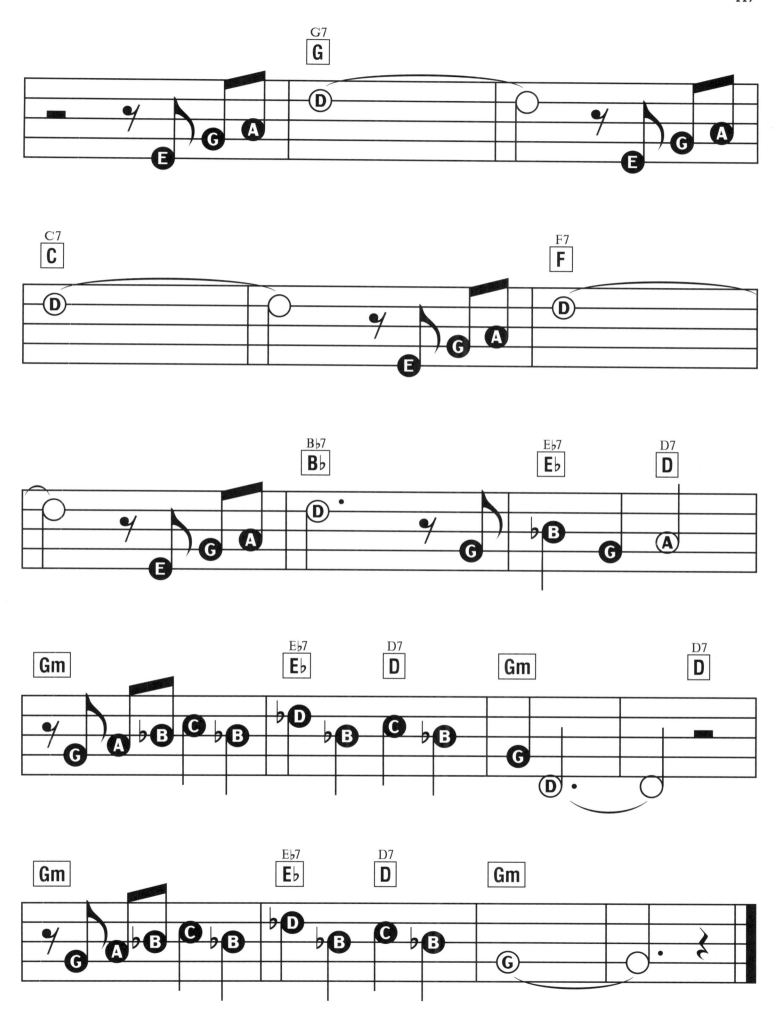

Up Jumped Spring

Registration 8
Rhythm: Jazz Waltz or Waltz

By Freddie Hubbard

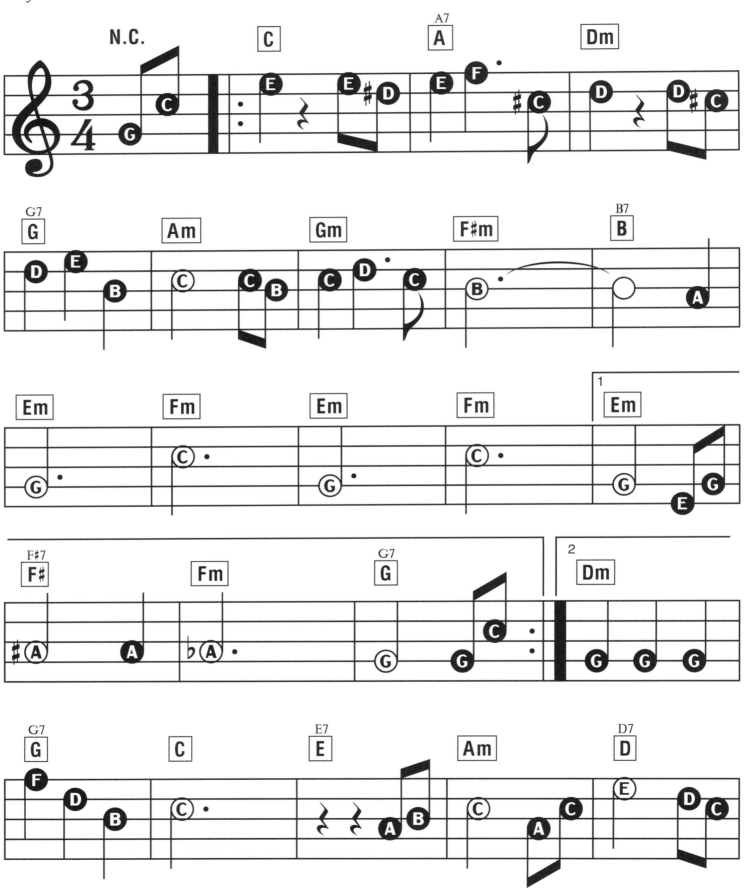

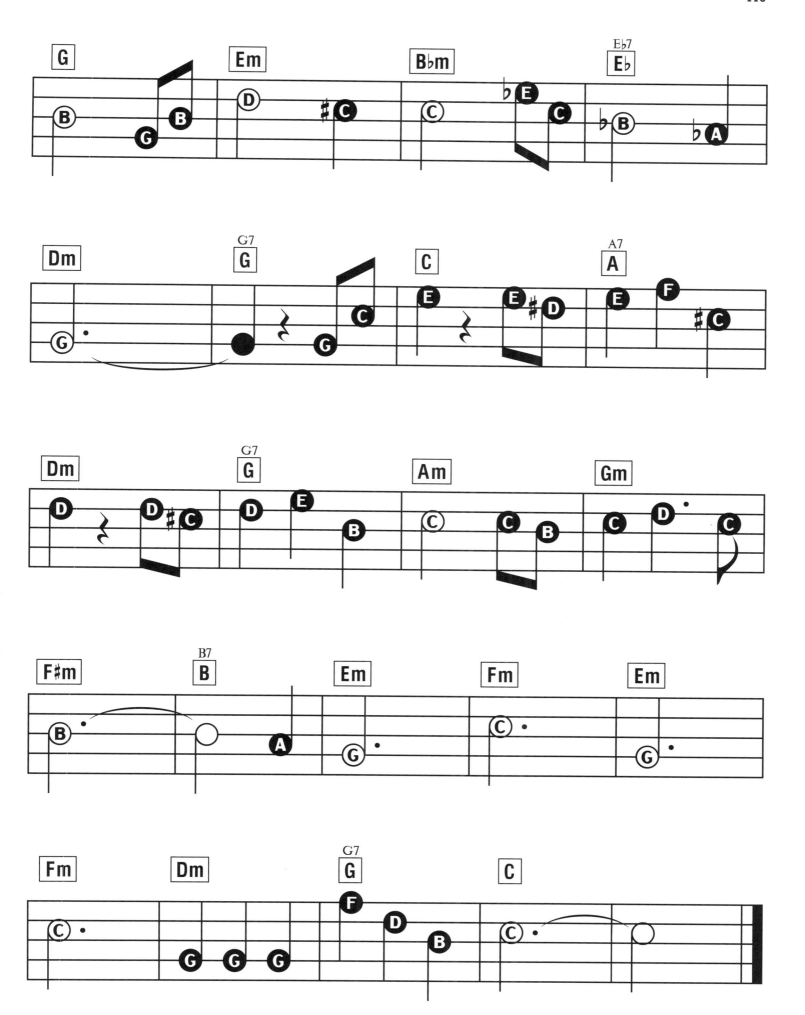

Warm Valley

Registration 8
Rhythm: Ballad

By Duke Ellington

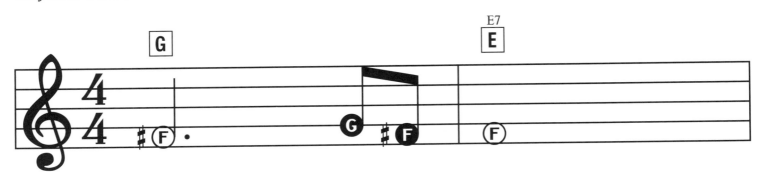

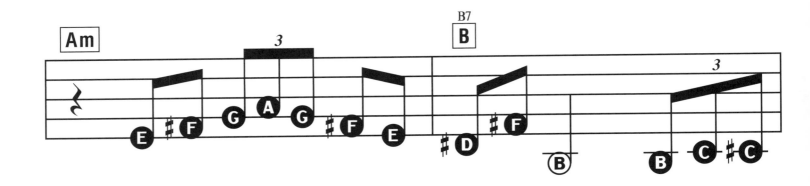

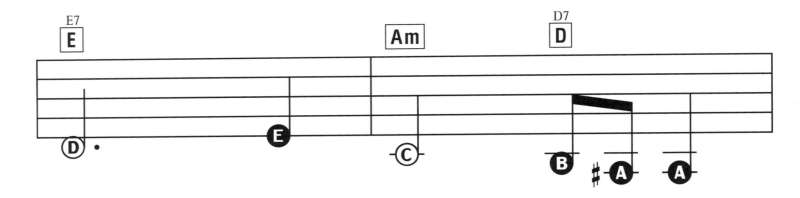

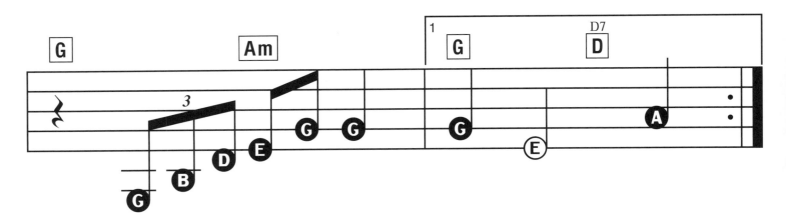

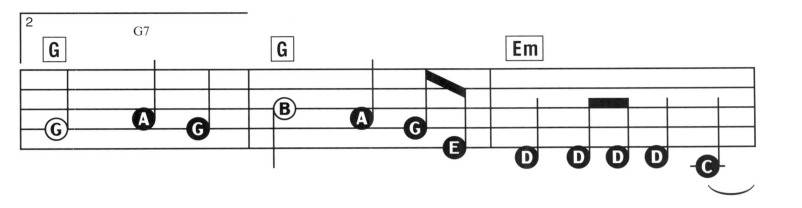

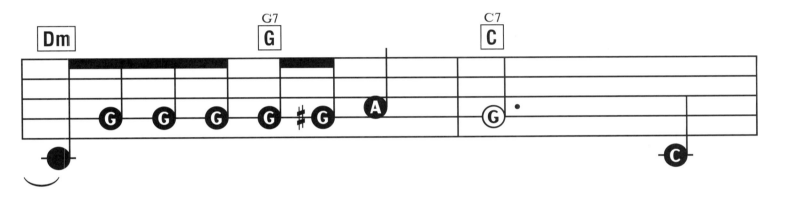

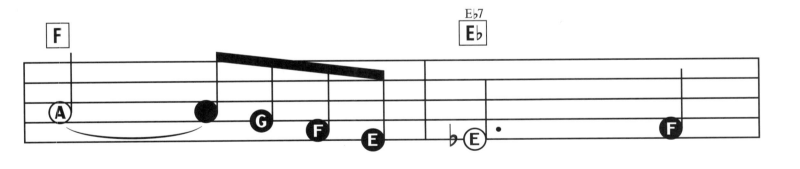

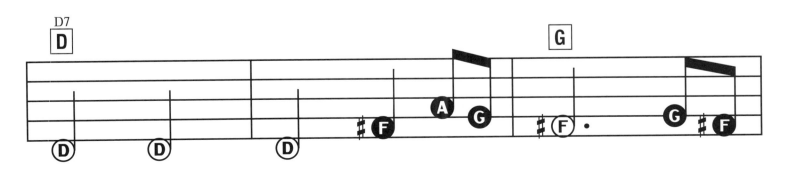

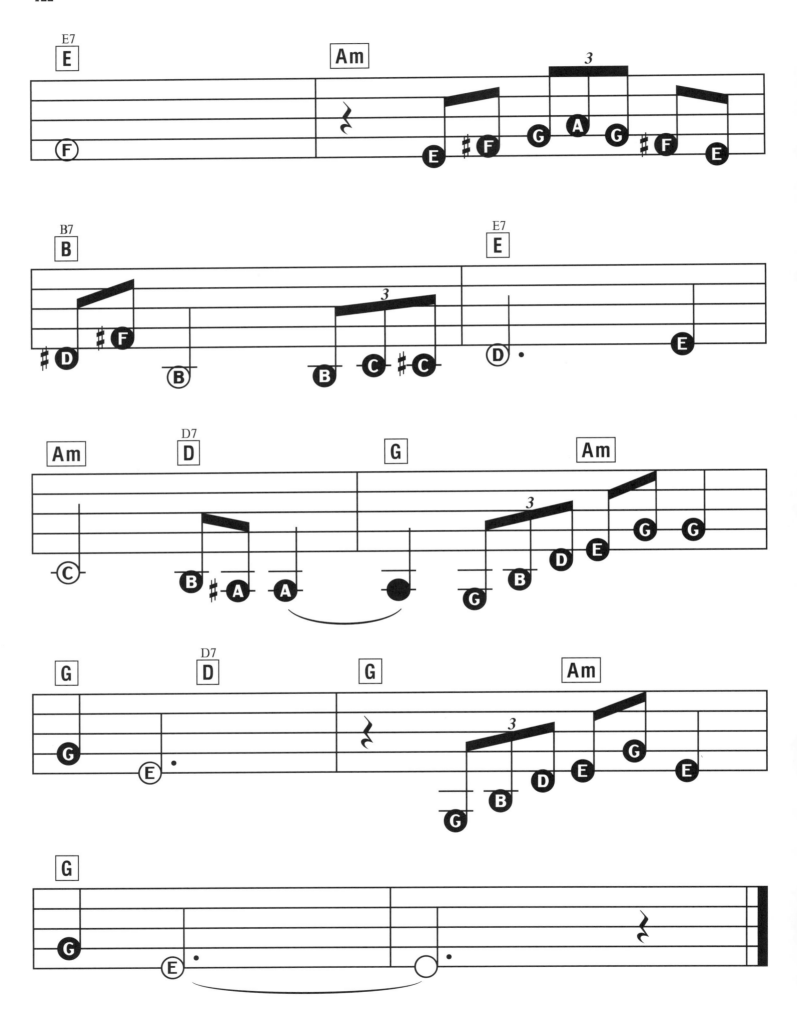

Well You Needn't
(It's Over Now)

Registration 8
Rhythm: Swing

Words by Mike Ferro
Music by Thelonious Monk

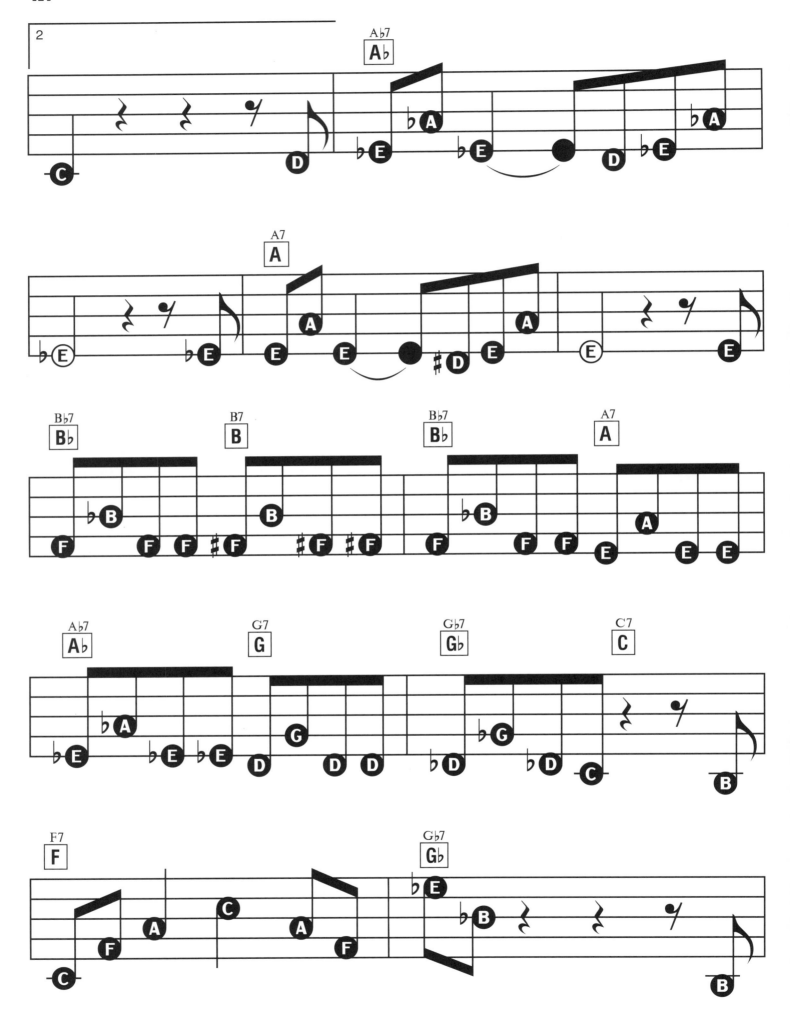

125

West Coast Blues

Registration 4
Rhythm: Jazz Waltz

By John L. (Wes) Montgomery

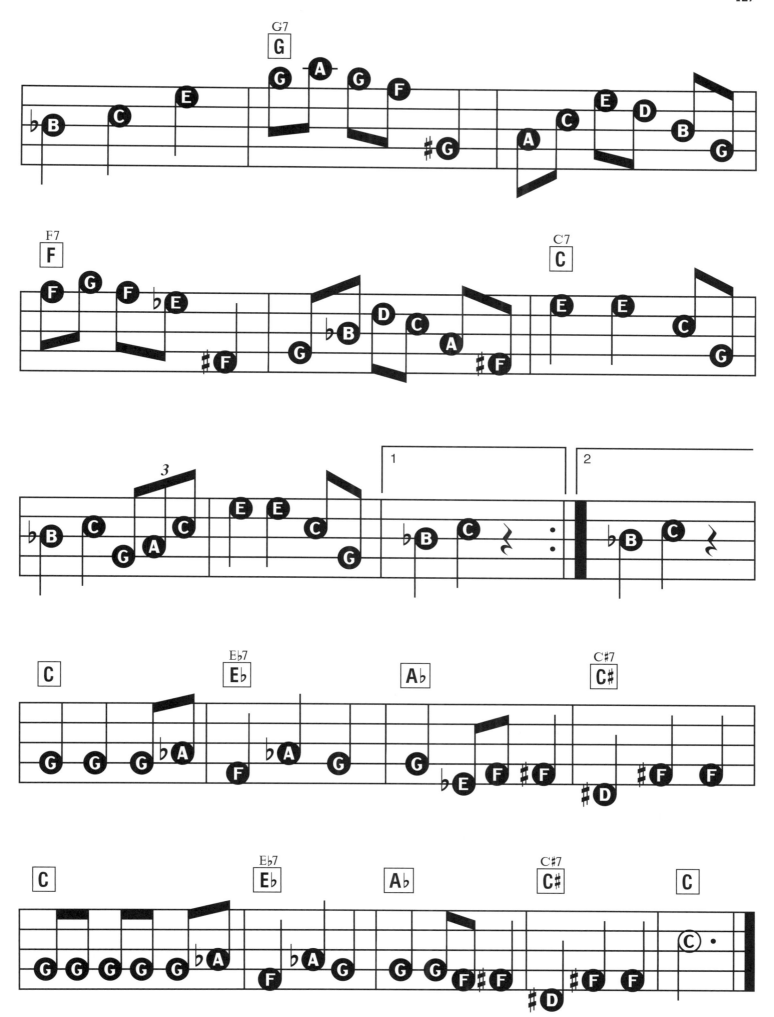

When Joanna Loved Me

Registration 1
Rhythm: Ballad

Words and Music by Robert Wells
and Jack Segal

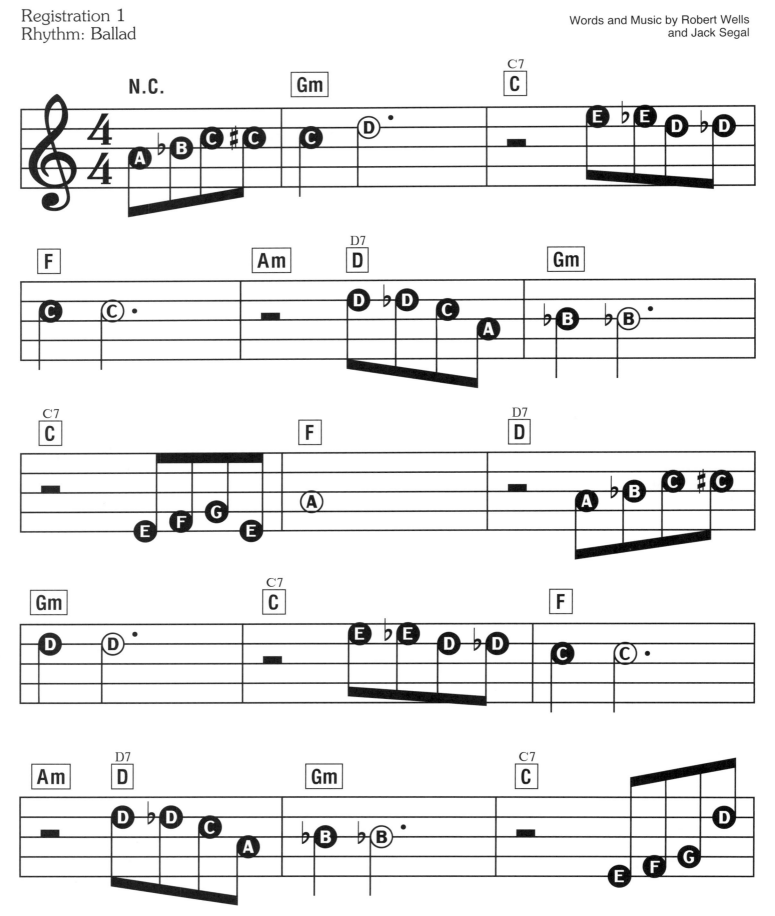

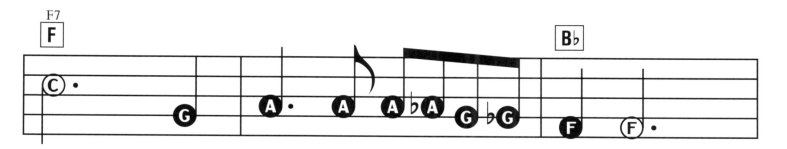

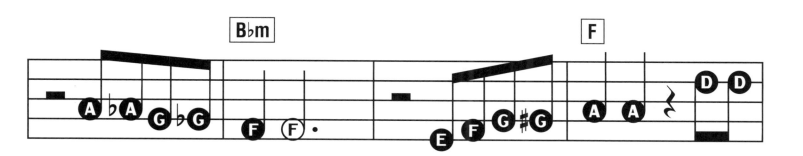

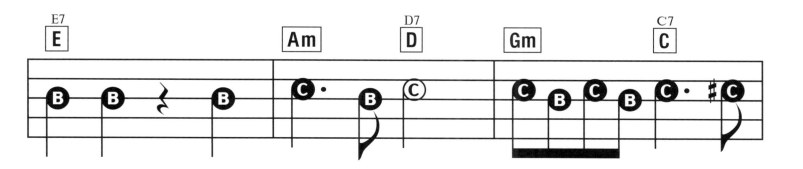

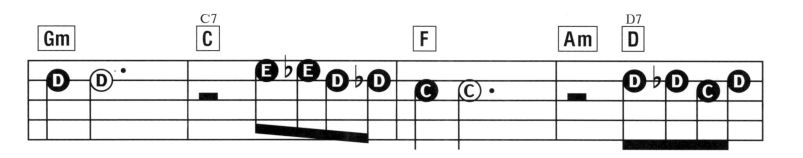

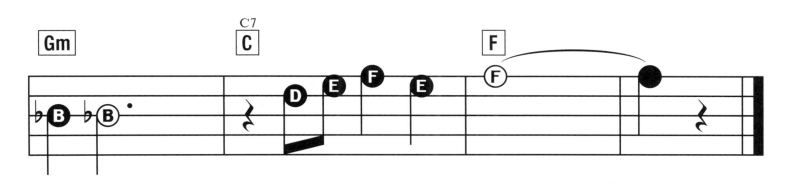

Whisper Not

Registration 2
Rhythm: Swing

By Benny Golson

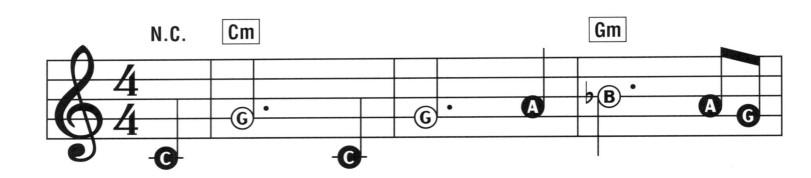

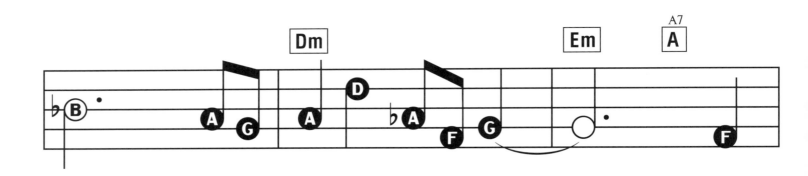

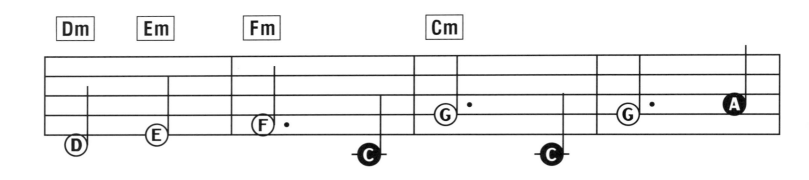

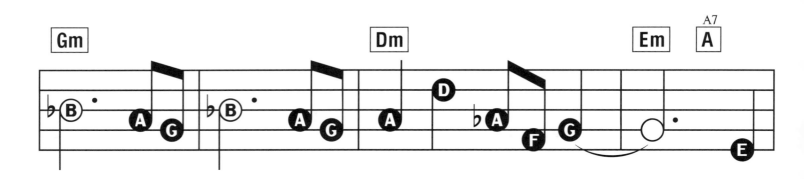

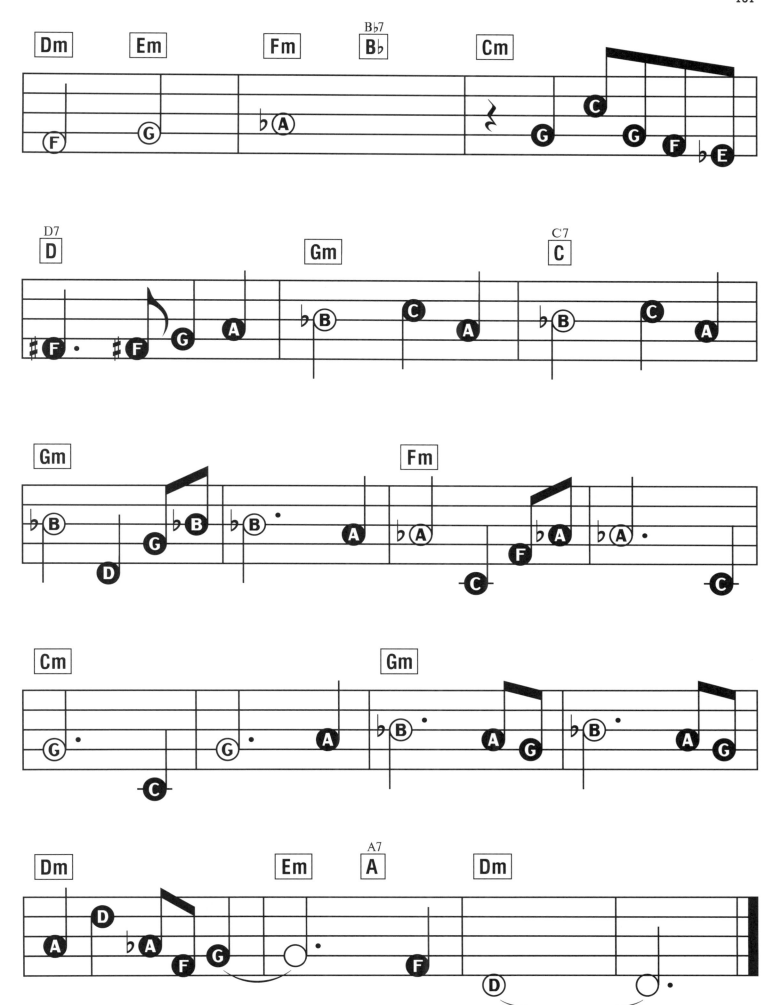

Woodyn' You

Registration 7
Rhythm: Swing

By Dizzy Gillespie

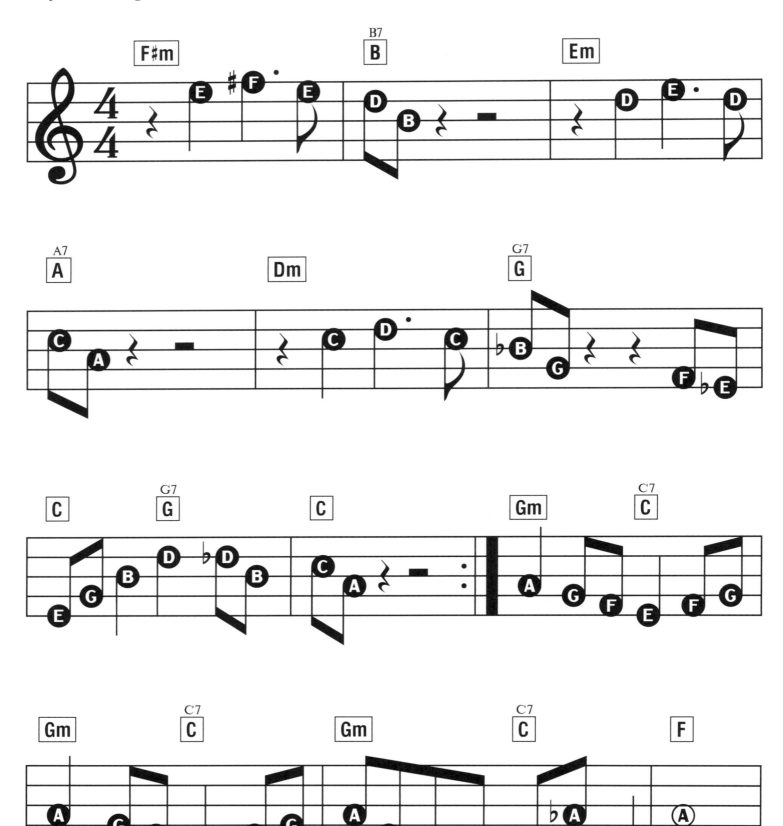

133

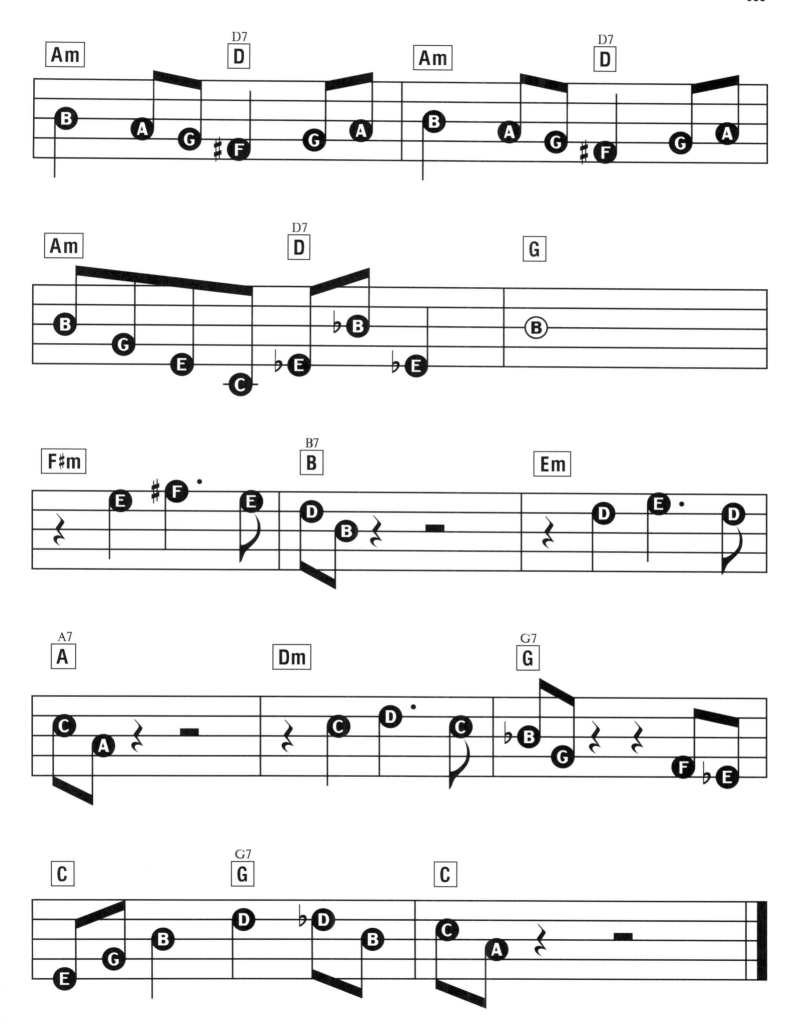

Work Song

Registration 8
Rhythm: Swing

By Nathaniel Adderley

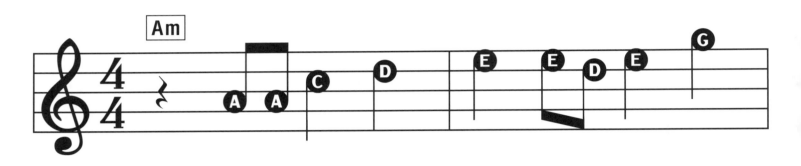

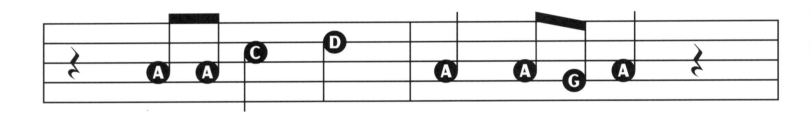

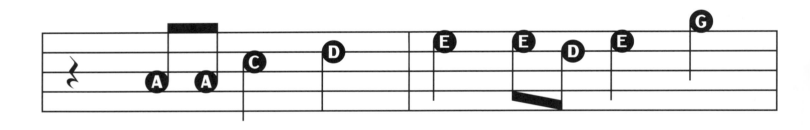

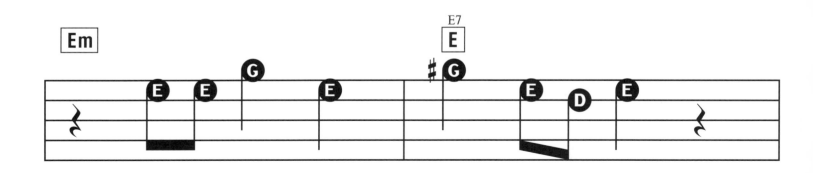

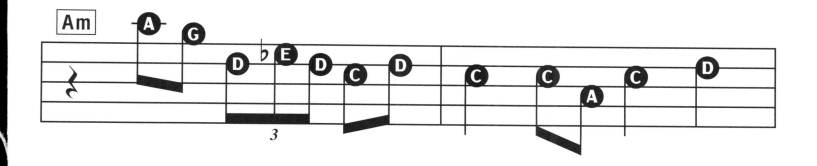

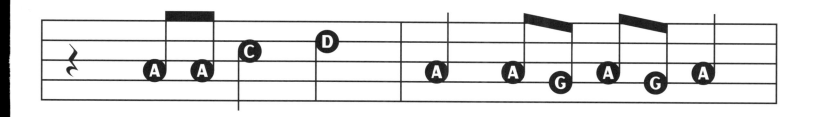

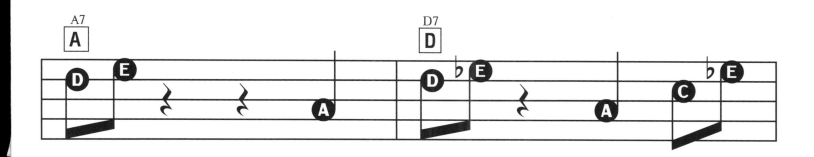

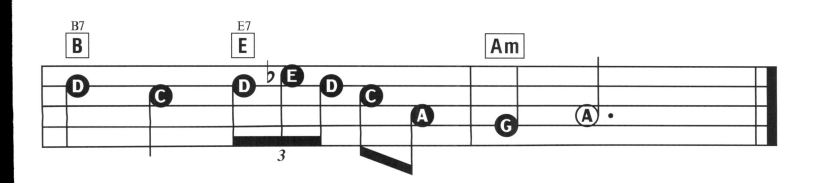

Registration Guide

- Match the Registration number on the song to the corresponding numbered category below. Select and activate an instrumental sound available on your instrument.

- Choose an automatic rhythm appropriate to the mood and style of the song. (Consult your Owner's Guide for proper operation of automatic rhythm features.)

- Adjust the tempo and volume controls to comfortable settings.

Registration

1	Mellow	Flutes, Clarinet, Oboe, Flugel Horn, Trombone, French Horn, Organ Flutes
2	Ensemble	Brass Section, Sax Section, Wind Ensemble, Full Organ, Theater Organ
3	Strings	Violin, Viola, Cello, Fiddle, String Ensemble, Pizzicato, Organ Strings
4	Guitars	Acoustic/Electric Guitars, Banjo, Mandolin, Dulcimer, Ukulele, Hawaiian Guitar
5	Mallets	Vibraphone, Marimba, Xylophone, Steel Drums, Bells, Celesta, Chimes
6	Liturgical	Pipe Organ, Hand Bells, Vocal Ensemble, Choir, Organ Flutes
7	Bright	Saxophones, Trumpet, Mute Trumpet, Synth Leads, Jazz/Gospel Organs
8	Piano	Piano, Electric Piano, Honky Tonk Piano, Harpsichord, Clavi
9	Novelty	Melodic Percussion, Wah Trumpet, Synth, Whistle, Kazoo, Perc. Organ
10	Bellows	Accordion, French Accordion, Mussette, Harmonica, Pump Organ, Bagpipes